SUCCESS WITH
REAL ESTATE MAILERS

JANINE SASSO

Copyright © 2021 by Janine Sasso

All rights reserved. No part of this book may be reproduced or used in any manner without written permission of the copyright owner except for the use of quotations in a book review. For more information, address: coaching@3KeysRealEstateGroup.com

FIRST EDITION

www.MailerMom.com

To Mason & Dylan

BEFORE WE DIVE IN

Mailer Mom - The free 5-Day Bootcamp

This is a free Training that I host!
There is No Cost, but I only run the bootcamp a few times a year!
So don't wait to get in on the next one!

"How to get your First (or Next) Successful Real Estate Mailer designed and sent off to print in less than a week WITHOUT paying Expensive Third-Party Services and Finally Generate Real Leads on Demand!"

This Works Even if you have never sent a Mailer for Generating Buyer & Seller Leads Before!

REGISTER NOW FOR THE NEXT BOOTCAMP!!
www.MailerMomBootcamp.com

Walk through the exact steps I take to get a new successful Mailer generated that sets listing appointments for me without dragging people through a sales pitch!

TABLE OF CONTENTS

INTRODUCTION 1

    The Problem..3

    MY GOAL FOR YOU 6

    The 6 C-Sale Cycle..8

    My Top 5 Reasons why mailer marketing works 11

    Time versus money..14

    The Road Ahead..18

CHAPTER 1: FOUNDATION THE BASIC PRINCIPLES FOR MAILERS..................21

    The 7 Stages of a Successful Real Estate Mailer 22

    The 3 Most Common Mailer Objectives..................................25

    10 Reasons people take actions 28

    3 Types of Lists - Who you mail to matters!............................30

    3 Types of Audiences...34

    Two types of mailers, lead generation and brand awareness versus lead nurture and sphere of influence mailers. 37

CHAPTER 2: MAILERS FOR LEAD GENERATION 39

    Five success keys for your mailer 40

    Lead Generation Mailers 56

    THE BLANKET..58

    BULLSEYE-TARGETING 60

    3 ways to use targeting for lead generation..........................62

    My Top 10 Seller Mailers - Get more leads and more listings........65

Theories for Just Listed/Just Sold/Under Contract/Coming soon Mailers...71

CHAPTER 3 MAILERS FOR LEAD NURTURE 73

The Fortune is in the Follow-up 74

Success Story Nurture 78

CHAPTER 4: THE NERDY CHAPTER 81

Direct Mail Statistics for 2021 82

Size of Postcard Mailers 84

PRINTING GUIDE 87

The Rules of 1-1-1 91

The Rule of 7 93

The Math behind mailers 96

THE 21st CENTURY DIFFERENCE 99

THE FAQs 103

Co-Marketing Opportunities - Your Vendors 113

Co-Branding and COMPLIANCE 115

THE ULTIMATE TACTIC - A MAGIC PILL SOLUTION 120

CHAPTER 5: RESOURCES 125

INTRODUCTION

"**P**ostcards for the win to generate 6-figures!" I thought I couldn't trust my ears! Did she just say, a piece of mail can bring in that much?

I sat dumbfounded in my chair at the seminar! How in the world can a piece of paper move people to take action? I had to get to the bottom of this! After all there were bills to pay and I was really enjoying spending all that time with my toddler at the park! Sending a piece of mail instead of making endless sales calls sounded so much better to me! Fast forward a short few years and I can honestly say: It's true, postcard marketing can generate you 6-figures in income! And in your hand you are holding the key discoveries on my journey. I am going to share with you inside this book, how you can increase the effectiveness of your postcard marketing to get more leads, higher opt-in rates and with that, more sales and more money to your bank account.

Sending a postcard seems to many people like an old-school strategy that is no longer effective. I want to let you know that those naysayers couldn't be more off when it comes to postcard marketing.

In today's day and age, where everything is going digital and you are competing like crazy for online advertisement space, it is now once again, the perfect opportunity for snail mail to make their debut and help you generate massive leads for your business.

Did you know that the consumer actually trusts businesses that are sending physical items in the mail much more than any other online business? Yes, it's true and I am taking you on a journey with direct mail statistics in a later chapter. But before I drop statistics and crazy numbers that will make your head spin on you, I want to cover some principles in the beginning along with what you can expect from this book. We all know it takes three things for a prospect to do business with us. They need to know us, they need to like us, and they need to trust us. Once we have those three components in place, a business transaction is much more likely.

If you picked up this book, thinking it's just going to talk about postcard mailer in the traditional old school way, I want to be very straightforward. This book is actually about mailer marketing in the 21st century. Print marketing in itself has existed for decades. Yet most agents have not implemented a more high level and technology advanced approach to mailers, leaving them with a low ROI and lots of frustration. This book has the mission to change that and help you develop a successful postcard/mailer campaign that will generate massive amounts of leads and listings, so you can continue building your real estate empire.

THE PROBLEM

When I first got licensed, I was as green as can be but after a few short months I started to gain rapid traction which catapulted me into the Top Producer Ranks pretty quickly. Yet I was still working a fulltime job that took up my day time hours in addition to being a mom. In 2019 I started looking for more support in my real estate business in the form of a coach. And what I found ended up laying the groundwork of what you are holding in your hands now. I was shocked that there wasn't much support out there for working moms, moms who are deciding to spend time with their children, to be there for all their milestones from the first step, to potty training and to kiss the scraped knee.

What I found is that many of the coaching approaches were centered around prospecting during regular business hours, which really conflicted with doctor appointments that I had to take my infant to, nap schedules, baseball games, vet appointments, and pretty much everything else called 'life'.

However, I also had this really big inner desire to grow my business into something that gave me the financial freedom, as well as the time freedom to do all those things while still earning a healthy six figure paycheck. And I'm glad to report that it's absolutely possible.

As I am writing this book, I am sitting next to my two kids on a campground and I am beyond grateful to have this time with them. And the reason I have this time with them is because I am able to take a step back from my business, knowing all my marketing is in place, doing the things that marketing is supposed to do, working for you while you are not actively working on it.

One of the things that I have in place are mailers and this is exactly what this book is going to be all about. I want you to discover how mailers have given me the opportunity to have leads calling me as opposed to me chasing them. I want you to discover how mailers have given me the freedom to run my business efficiently from any part of town and most of all, I want you to discover for yourself what's possible and to reach your own full potential!

In this book, I'm going to share with you one of the most important pillars to my business. I built a lot of my business based on postcard mailers for the fact that I was able to put my marketing pieces in place after hours, in my case, after bedtime. And during the day I had leads coming in that I was then able to nurture and convert into buyers and sellers.

But let me backtrack a few years. There was no silver spoon feeding me.

When I started out in real estate, I tried a lot of things. I've tried open houses. I've tried networking. I've tried flyers, Facebook groups, and social media. And, because I didn't have a big sphere, I needed to always be a little bit more creative than the average agent. So, when I first started, I had zero marketing money, meaning I did not realize, coming freshly out of licensing class, that this business of mine needed investing into. And, thinking back now, I can honestly say I did invest into it, just not monetarily. When I first started out, I invested my time into it and while we are going to talk about mailers in this book, I also wanted you to understand that I did not start out with mailers because, frankly put, the budget wasn't there. (And if this is you, keep reading because I am going to reveal to you an absolutely free strategy that uses the principles of Mailers, but in a free way! And who doesn't like free?)

Before I start and jump into it, let me introduce myself real quick. My name is Janine Sasso. I am an active real estate agent and team leader. The reason I bring it up here is because I want you to understand that this book is not written based on theory. This book is written because I understand what is happening in today's marketplace. I am in the trenches, just like you. I've marketed to sellers in order to get more listings and I understand where the pain points are for our buyers. I'm also a mom of two young kids, a dog owner, a team leader, as well as a course creator at The Hyper Local Real Estate Agent. You can join our free Facebook Group for Real Estate Agents here: www.facebook.com/groups/thehyperlocalagent

So, thank you so much for picking up the book. And let's dive in and discover how mailers can be used in your business to help you gain the freedom and the income you desire.

MY GOAL FOR YOU

The goal of this book is really simple. I want to remove the guesswork for mailers, and I want you to discover a six figure income strategy that generates leads and listings, cuts out expensive third-party services, also known as the middleman, and let's you build a solid lead gen pillar for your real estate business.

Many have said that my method is a lot more of a DIY method. And I do agree to some extent. My goal is for you to understand how something works, because once you master it, you can hand over the reins of creation and implementation to somebody you hire or outsource. However, the skills that you are going to learn are going to be invaluable to you. And this is regardless of any market.

I'm a big believer in the fact that skill acquisition is one of the most important things a business owner can do. Once we acquire a skill, we're able to understand if the job we hire out for it is done in a way that is adequate.

I want to impact the real estate agent that has been in the same boat as me, the real estate agent that is sitting at home wondering where do I get a babysitter in order for me to show my buyers that house without bringing my children along, the real estate agent that's wondering how do I get to build a profitable business while also being a good parent. And, honestly, this alone means you are a good parent if you are wondering how you can be a good parent.

So, this is for all the agents out there that do not have time to prospect from nine to five because they have life happen. This is for all the agents out there that want to be there for the kids, grandkids or their own parents, yet they also want to have a business that they can be proud of and that's meant to support them financially in order for them to be with the most important people.

Now, what is this book not? This book is not going to be filled with filler words. It is written to make sure I get the point across in the shortest amount of time. My goal is not for you to spend hours and hours reading a book, and then having no time to implement it. I want you to get straight down to the chapter where you will find the most valuable information and implement it, so you can be successful as quickly as possible. After reading the book, I believe you will have all the tools necessary to do postcard marketing the right way, which will give you more leads and more listings.

THE 6 C-SALE CYCLE

Let me introduce you to a concept I call "My 6 C Sale Cycle". This little wheel is truly the framework of my business and has built my business to its first 6-figures. The cycle shows the journey of a customer as they interact with us as their real estate advisor. The cycle is heavily built on bringing value to your customer/client throughout the entire journey that they are with us. The very first thing we need to do is to attract them to us and our business. By bringing awareness to our business and what we do for a living, we are able to create opportunities. This is why it is so important to NOT be a secret agent.

STEP #1: CREATE

The first step in our customer journey is to create awareness in our customers that they have a need for our services. By creating this internal desire, consumers are now open to the idea of our services and what we have to offer.

STEP #2: CAPTURE

Once we create that desire/awareness in our potential customers, it's time to filter out the ones that are raising their hand to go to the next level with us. There are many ways to capture a lead. You can go old school with physical sign-ins and new school with automated lead capture techniques, and of course anything in between!

STEP #3: CULTIVATE

Let's build a connection! Similar to a farmer cultivating his field to receive a full harvest, we have to cultivate our customers into clients (and ideally raving fans!). Provide value to your customers any opportunity you get.

STEP #4: CONVERT

This step is your foot in the door. We want to get face to face with our prospect in order for us to deliver our buyer consultation or sit down for a listing appointment. Building a relationship is not instant but you are almost there!

STEP #5: CUSTOMER EXPERIENCE

This is a crucial step in our cycle as it can lead to an abundance of referral business if done right! Making our customer feel like they are our #1 priority is a lost art. Remember that buying or selling a house might be the norm for you from a professional standpoint, but your customer comes to you with a once in a blue moon event. Just recently did I hear from an agent that said she got fired by her buyers because she was too pessimistic about the market. Be aware on how this might potentially be received by your clients. Be honest, yet enthusiastic at all times is truly the best rule to live by.

STEP #6: CAPITALIZE

And here is your big payoff! You have completed the first cycle for your client and we are closing the deal. But that doesn't mean this is the end of the station. We are going to create the next desire/awareness when the time comes. It might be several years until we get to go through a consequent cycle with our client, but eventually there might be the desire to upsize, downsize or purchase investment property.

MY TOP 5 REASONS WHY MAILER MARKETING WORKS

Many people think that a real estate agent's job is to sell houses (or help their buyers purchase them for that matter). However, this is merely the product of something else that a real estate agent should be doing. As a sales position we have to start looking further upstream. What should be our main focus is getting in front of new prospects. As often as possible. By continuing to expand our reach and the people we interact with, we are going to increase our chances to gain a lead. Leads to a real estate agent are like the blood in your body. They are absolutely essential. Wonder what this top producing agent is doing to gain the business they are getting? They are getting in front of more people than the average agent! And it really does not matter with which tactic you are using to accomplish this goal, as long as the objective is met. Personally, I love Mailers. They are the most efficient way to get in front of as many people as possible with the least amount of effort. I am creating a desire in them once they receive my mailer. So that being said, let me share with you my top 5 reasons mailer marketing is a magical solution.

IT DOESN'T HAVE TO BE OPENED

First up, a mailer does not have to be opened like a regular piece of mail, such as a letter or even an email. Your message is right there in the front. A prospect gets to see it with the least amount of effort. And while you might think opening a letter or email doesn't take much effort, I want to remind you that we gladly take the drive-up option as opposed to walking into the business. Instead of walking into Target, we pick ther drive-up, instead of going grocery shopping we select Instacart Delivery, instead of buying light bulbs at the local store, we order them from Amazon. It doesn't take much but it's much more convenient this way. We have to display less effort and with that it's becoming the logical choice. How many times have you looked at an envelope and decided right there and then that it was junk without even opening it? With Mailers you can rest assured that you are at least leaving an impression with your lead.

TRUST

The second reason that speaks for mailer marketing is the fact that prospects trust printed advertising the most. Let's assume you are looking to buy a car. If I give you the choice between buying from an online store you've never heard of and buying from a trusted local store, most prospects will pick the local store for the trust factor that comes with it. A house is even more expensive than a car and prospects will want to know that they are in good hands!

ACTION TAKERS

The third reason mailer marketing works is for the fact that 79% of prospects are ready to take action once they opt in. In contrast online real estate leads are many times further up the pipeline, with current data statistics suggesting that the average length of a pipeline for an online lead is upwards of 2 years!

HYPER LOCAL MARKETING

The fourth reason I think mailer marketing is absolutely amazing is for the fact that you can get hyper local and really niche down where you want to be at. In a world of online advertisement and the restrictions that come along with it, saturating a 15 mile radius on a Facebook Ad has gotten quite expensive as well as competitive. Of course you can 'call out' your ideal lead with things such as ad copy, images and interests but why make it more complicated than necessary, right?

LONGEVITY

My fifth reason why mailer marketing is definitely something all agents should consider and the number one reason that mailers are most often overlooked is this: Mailers can live on for a loooong time after being sent. Have you heard about the story of the drawer filled with postcards? An agent went on a listing appointment and the home owner showed him how he had saved all the mailers that the agent had sent dating years back! I don't think that has happened with an email ever!

TIME VERSUS MONEY

> *"Time is more valuable than money. You can get more money, but you cannot get more time!"*
> *- Jim Rohn*

The very first principle in real estate is really simple. We all have two resources and we always have to choose between spending one of them. Either we spend our time or we spend our money.

When I was brand new in real estate, I did not have a lot of files to juggle or a lot of calls to make. My lead database was little. So, all those things that a busy agent does, I didn't have to do because I wasn't busy. YET!

What I had to spare and granted, I didn't have to spare a lot of it, was my time. I decided that the first thing I was going to do was to invest my most precious resource, which is time. It started out with 100 flyers, my child in a stroller and a pair of really good walking shoes. I delivered flyers in order for me to generate leads with my baby in the stroller while taking a walk. Two flies with one squat, or however the saying goes.

When I started, it was slow going and it was time consuming, but I was determined to see if I could get a payoff from my strategy. After all, it wasn't costing me any money! Open houses were on my agenda very early on as well. They didn't cost me anything.. I've done a lot of them to the point where I could probably give you the blueprint on how to host a mega open house event that will drive massive leads to you. But I'll save that for another time.

When I picked up a lead from my open house event, I would get clear on their criteria. And if it was something that was small enough of an area for me to target, I would print out my flyers and I would hit the pavement.

Here is when I developed my two-step flyer process that rests on the foundational principles of mailers, many of which I am going to cover in this book. Let me share with you though what this two-step process looks like. This tactic alone is something you can implement right away without relying on a marketing budget. No need to spend money on postcards, as long as you are willing to invest your time and bring flyers around to homes as a cost-effective alternative.

So, what did I do after talking with a prospect at the open house? Let me give you one example of a conversation I remember. The visitor to my open house was extremely focused on that particular community of townhomes. But only townhomes that had three bedrooms, which were already only a few of them to a lot of them. Next I went to the tax records. I filtered out all the addresses that had those matching criteria. I printed out a bunch of flyers that said I had a buyer looking for this specific kind of home. If they were even slightly considering a move, I would love for them to get touch. I told them they'd be surprised how much the buyer was willing to pay for their home. I had a really high response rate from this one already, but that didn't stop me from going one step further. And I really think that one step further was where I saw the spike in the response rate.

About a week later, I went into the same community again with the second flyer. My second flyer had something on it along the lines of, "Hey, I'm sorry, I missed you. I was just in your neighborhood following up on my flyer from about a week ago. My buyer is still looking and I'd love to find him the perfect home. By the way, this is my contact information. Don't hesitate to reach out." And the responses went through the roof.

That two-step system right there allowed me to get in touch with a lot of people for virtually nothing. I used my office printer to get all my flyers printed. I used my office supplies such as the rubber bands. So, all I had to invest on my own was my time.

So, fast-forward to today, and I am currently farming an area with 5,000 mailers a month. Now, this is not going to be the end of my station. This is merely a milestone on the path to grow even further. But did I go from a hundred flyers to 5,000 postcards? Absolutely not. I went from a hundred flyers to 400 postcards, to 800 postcards, to 1200 postcards, to 1600 postcards, to 2000 postcards, to 3000, and then to 5,000.

So, the truth is, you need to start somewhere, and regardless of where you start, the biggest thing is, I want you to make sure you can be consistent with these efforts.

And now that I'm getting busier with files as well, my resource of time is getting smaller. However, my resource of money is getting larger. So, there is a tipping scale where you will invest more off one thing than the other.

And there is nobody else that knows your business better than you. So, check out your own business and determine where your best starting point would be. If you're not brand new to the business and you have a marketing budget, then maybe you're going to start with mailings right away. Maybe you are in the middle and will spend both of your resources equally. Maybe you are brand new and you just picked up this book, because you decided it was going to be a great strategy for you to try out. I hope you find some value in some of the free strategies that I'm sprinkling for you in these pages.

THE ROAD AHEAD

> *"It's always best to start at the beginning and follow the yellow brick road".*
> *- The Wizard of Oz*

What's a trip to the mountains without a compass? A road trip without a GPS and a plan? Chances are you are leaving a lot of things up to chance and will not reach your destination.

G - Goal: What's your big goal?
P - Plan: How will you get there (Milestones)
S - Strategy: What are the tactics you will use to reach your goal(s)?

This is a simple framework to tackle anything inside your business and life. Most people fail because they are trying to make things more complicated than what they need to be. Not you! I know you will see the path that is laid out in front of you and by following the yellow brick road, you will find success!

This book is divided into 5 components!

1. Foundation
2. Mailers for Lead Generation
3. Mailers for Lead Nurture
4. The Nerdy Chapter - your most burning questions answered!
5. Resources

Each of these chapters can be used as a reference guide throughout your mailer journey. I hope that you keep this book handy, not just for your mailer marketing but see the value in the frameworks I am sharing with you! Some of these frameworks are marketing principles that are not taught in real estate licensing class. No wonder our failure rate is so high! My goal is to help more agents find the fulfillment they are seeking when they set out to get their license. For me it was the fact that I wanted to earn a decent living while being with my kids through all their major milestones. Entrepreneurship is seldomly the reason people set out to get their license. Reasons are much more centered around our core values and why we perceive real estate as the ideal solution to our financial and family goals. If this book accomplishes just that for you, it was well worth the time writing it.

Now I want you to read the next pages with an open mind. This book is going to dive deep on how to use mailers to generate more leads for your real estate business.

For access to all the free Resources and Trainings mentioned in this book, please go to:

www.MailerMomResources.com

CHAPTER 1

FOUNDATION THE BASIC PRINCIPLES FOR MAILERS

THE 7 STAGES OF A SUCCESSFUL REAL ESTATE MAILER

> *"The secret of getting ahead is getting started!"* - Mark Twain

There are several stages to a successful mailer. And I want to go over these with you. Once you know what milestone to look out for, it's going to be a lot easier to forge your path to success.

Stage 1: Design the mailer.

This part is probably the most crucial one because what you mail matters. However, the fact that you should mail something, is also very important.

I see so many agents being confused with what they should send, to the point where they actually never send anything because they are hung up on that question. And no worries, I'm going to give you a lot of inspiration in a later chapter as well as a complete framework on what should be on the mailers in order to trigger a response.

Stage 2: Send the mailer.

You'd be surprised how many people actually design a mailer and then never push the send button. Sending the mailer is probably the most crucial step. So, I want to go over with you, how you can make sure you send a mailer and not only am I going to show you where to get it printed, how to select the right size, but I also want to make sure that you are getting the most cost effective rate for your mailings. So, we will talk about that later in this book as well.

Stage 3: Receive a lead and build your pipeline.

This is the part where I want you to be super excited, because you can finally say your mailer generated a lead. But no worries, we don't want to stop just here. We actually dig deeper into the data to see what landed in our 'invisible pipeline'. We will talk about this most overlooked pipeline later on in this book and how you can tap into a hidden source for deals that most agents overlook.

Stage 4: Set the appointment.

Time to celebrate. You have a schedule listing appointment or buyer consultation on your calendar from your mailer. This is something to celebrate. But this also means it is time to spring into action and start working on building up your authority as to why you are the only logical choice for your lead to hire.

Stage 5: Go on the appointment.

It's not enough to just set the appointment or even go on it. We are looking for the result: A listing appointment that secures the listing or a buyer consultation that gets the buyer to sign with you is crucial. I personally use an irresistible listing appointment presentation that leaves no room for second thoughts for my sellers.

Stage 6: Get the listing or the buyer agreement.

Just going on the appointment is not enough, we want to make sure that our lead signs on the dotted line. You want to be able to overcome objections and clearly articulate your unique value proposition as to why people should hire you.

Stage 7: Close the transaction.

And this is where we're going to celebrate all the efforts you've put into your business so far. Closing the transaction is the final piece of the puzzle. It is the product of all your efforts over the last few weeks or even months! Pat yourself on the shoulder! A job well done!

THE 3 MOST COMMON MAILER OBJECTIVES

> *"If the plan does not work, change the plan not the goal!"*
> *- unknown*

Let me share with you the most common mailer objectives, and we're going to go and categorize them from easy to hard. Every mailer we send has an objective. If we are sending mailers without a purpose, we are wasting our money. So when every mailer needs to have a purpose, what should this purpose be? The number one mistake I see most agents make is simply using their mailers as a form of marketing their listing, not so much for business building. But this is the magic of mailers. Mailers are an amazing tool to build your business. So without further delay, let's talk about the three mailer objectives.

Mailer objective #1: Lead Generation - Level: EASY

It almost sounds like a no-brainer that a book about success with real estate mailers is telling you what the number one mailer objective is lead generation.

But what is lead generation? The goal for lead generation is simply for you to gain a contact with a name and a way to contact them. That might be a phone number, an address, or an email. Generating a lead is actually one of the easiest objectives that you can accomplish with your mailer.

Mailer objective #2: Registrations - Level: MEDIUM

The second mailer objective that you could be aiming for is registrations. You might think: What would I want them to register for? Let me give you some examples. You could promote an event, or offer potential clients a seat at your buyer seminar or seller seminar. There are quite a few different ways to use mailers and increase registrations. For example, I actually host an annual neighborhood garage sale that I do send out one mailer, which prompts people to sign up to participate with their address as well as their email. This is just one of the ways that I was able to build my email list of targeted neighborhood residents that know, like, and trust me very efficiently without trying to sell them only on real-estate-related conversations. If we are in the relationship building business, then where is our focus on relationships?

Mailer objective #3: Appointment Setting - Level: HARD

This is the one that most people use, and it's actually the hardest one of all, which makes your mailer campaigns many times not profitable. The most used call to action is call or contact me. Are you guilty of this one? Don't worry! You are not alone! And honestly, I get it. We've been told to put this on marketing pieces for as long as we can remember. However, in this day and age, we have so many other tools available with a lower barrier of entry that we really should consider other forms of prompting our leads to take action.

For example, instead of saying, "Just call me," you could also have a website leading to an appointment scheduler online. This is a great way to put the lead back in charge of when and how they want to communicate with you.

Now, keep in mind, this is the hardest objective to accomplish. And if you are looking to get the highest return on your money, a lead generation mailer is a better way to go.

10 REASONS PEOPLE TAKE ACTIONS

> *You don't have to be great to start hit you have to start to be great!*
> *- Zig Ziglar*

I want to give you a framework of the top 10 reasons why people will take action on something.

These 10 reasons are based on the psychology of what makes us humans do something. Might this be to take action, buy something, or opt into something to become, oh I don't know, lets say, a lead for a real estate agent? Action is inspired by an internal drive that is triggered by one or more of the following:

1. Make money
2. Save money
3. Save time
4. Avoid effort
5. Escape mental or physical pain
6. Get more comfort
7. Attain better health or hygiene
8. Gain praise
9. Feel more loved

10. Gain popularity or social status.

And here is the secret sauce: If your real estate mailer (or any kind of marketing) can incorporate more than one desire, the higher your conversion for your leads is going to be! When your message becomes the most desired solution to a problem, you will inspire action in a prospect

I suggest you keep this list very dear to your heart. This is exactly why people decide on buying a home. This is exactly why people decide they want to opt in and become a lead. And if this list is not making sense to you quite yet, hang on. Later on in this book, you will discover how these 10 pillars are going to be the key that will help you unlock massive leads for your lead generation efforts with postcard mailers.

3 TYPES OF LISTS - WHO YOU MAIL TO MATTERS!

> *You can't build a reputation on what you are going to do!*
> *- Henry Ford*

There are three types of lists that we can utilize when it comes to sending mailers. And I want to make it easy for you with this book by simply selecting the list that will work best for your plans with mailers. So let's dive in. What are the three types of lists that you could be utilizing to send mail?

Sphere of influence (SOI) List

The first option is of course, your sphere of influence, people that you know and that have done business with you. This list in general is generally one of the smaller lists. It is also a list that is used to continue staying in front of people.

As you will learn in the later chapters, you will need to select if you are sending a mailer for lead generation or if you are sending a mailer for lead nurture. Your SOI list should receive your lead nurture mailers. This is how simple this is. Staying in front of your sphere once a month with a lead nurture mailer is really a cost-effective way to retain a past client or to demonstrate your level of expertise to your friends and family as a real estate agent.

Targeted Lists

The next list you could use is a targeted list. A targeted list, for example, is something you can pull in the tax records when you filter for attributes such as length of ownership, style of home, basement or no basement, how many bedrooms, certain square footage, specific floor on a building, or whatever else you want to filter for. Using a targeted list has the benefit of being much more efficient for your message that you're trying to convey.

A targeted list is typically also more expensive to send mail to as you are cherry picking the homes you want to target. Where can you get these lists? You can get these lists from your title company or from the tax records, which should be accessible to you as a real estate agent. There are also services out there where you can purchase lists. However, I would expand on your free options first before you purchase these lists from another provider.

EDDM Routes

The third list option I want to cover is a tool offered through the United States Postal Office. You know that every mailman has a set route that they deliver to each and every day. And here's the thing. You can utilize the mailman's already existing routes through a system called Every Door Direct Mail. The cool thing about this list is the fact that it is extremely cost-effective to reach your target mailing address. The drawback, you are bound to select the entire route the mailman covers and cannot cherry pick the addresses.

Personally, I think this is a great way to incorporate geographic farming as it will help you keep your costs down while also building brand awareness with your mail pieces. It's important to note that the demographic on these mailing routes will vary widely, which also means that you will not be able to send out a mailer that addresses everybody's pain points like a targeted mailer would. What do I mean by this? Maybe your mailer is hinting on the fact that they need to buy a bigger house and you're sending this to a townhome community. Well, what if somebody on this route actually just came from a single family home and was downsizing into a townhome? The marketing message couldn't be more far off.

So again, be mindful of what your goal is and who you are trying to reach with your mailer message. I want to give you a bonus tip when it comes to the EDDM routes. You can actually check out the EDDM routes and get detailed information on the demographic of that specific mailing route based on the last census poll. The reason I think this is really helpful is because it shows you what the majority of homes on the routes are composed of. Maybe 45% of the owners on that specific route are between 50 and 70-years-old. I would tailor my message to fit the majority of recipients on that route, such as upsizing/downsizing to receive a potential lead. You can access the Every Door Direct Mail tool through the official website of the United States Postal Service or by simply typing in this link here: www.usps.com/business/every-door-direct-mail.htm

So which of these lists should you utilize? And the answer is it depends. Your SOI should receive something from you in general as these are people that already know you and like you and in many cases have done business with them.

So in my opinion, you have the targeted and the EDDM routes as two of the options for your lead generation mailers. Which one you choose is absolutely up to you. One of them, which is the targeted list, will be more expensive, but you'll be able to tailor your message a lot more specifically to your ideal lead. The EDDM routes can also convey the message and filter out your ideal leads, but are much less targeted. However these mailers can help build your brand in a geographic farm through saturation.

3 TYPES OF AUDIENCES

> *"Small deeds done are better than great deeds planned!"*
> *- Peter Marshall*

Let's talk about what's an audience and why does it matter? We define an audience as somebody that we are trying to engage. Somebody that is considering doing business with us in the future. Now their level of engagement is characterized by temperature. We will discuss these below next.

COLD

> *Cold – What would the conversation be like with people who know they have a problem, but they have no clue a solution even exists.*

A cold audience is somebody that is somewhat problem aware but they are not solution aware. They are online or offline until we grab their attention with our message. For a cold audience, our job is to make them solution aware. Once somebody is solution aware, we can slowly start presenting the solution to them and making them interested in what we have to say. In which case we wouldn't move them down to a warm audience.

So how does this work for mailers? I am sending a mailer for lead generation purposes into a geographic farm, through the means of an EDDM route. A potential lead sees this and says, "Oh my gosh, it says there are 90 things you need to do to get your home ready for sale." They are now becoming solution aware. They can collect their guide in which case they are raising their hand. And now they are getting moved to the next phase, which would be the warm audience.

Warm

> *Warm – What would the conversation be like with someone who is aware they have a problem, but not aware of you?*

Next is the warm audience and this is where we want to build relationships. A warm lead is somebody that has expressed an interest and is interested in what we have to say, to present or even to sell. Many of the warm audiences or warm leads are checking us out to see if they are aligning with what we are presenting. A warm audience is typically part of a lead nurture mailer campaign.

Hot

> *Hot – What would be the conversation with someone who knows who you are and what you do?*

If somebody is a hot prospect, a hot audience, they are ready to act now, take action and list the house right away or come and do a buyer consultation, look at houses, purchase a house, etc. These are generally people that are ready to pull the trigger. Now, wouldn't it be nice if we encounter somebody that's a hot prospect? In an ideal world; however, this happens only a few times throughout your real estate career. Most people are looking for a little bit more interaction before they select a service provider. But if we have a hot audience, it's important to present them with opportunities to connect with us. Invite them to your events, open houses, schedule an appointment or call. Give them the opportunity to go from lead to client.

TWO TYPES OF MAILERS, LEAD GENERATION AND BRAND AWARENESS VERSUS LEAD NURTURE AND SPHERE OF INFLUENCE MAILERS.

> *"A comfort zone is a beautiful place but nothing ever grows there!"*
> *- unknown*

Most people think postcard mailers have only one purpose, which is to market their listings. However, this is actually not the case. If I spend marketing money, I want to make sure I get the most bang for my buck. And therefore, I'm going to be differentiating between two types of mailers that your business has.

The first mailer is meant to generate leads and build brand awareness. Those mailers are sent to cold audiences who don't know you, you don't have their contact information, and you're trying to establish trust with them so that they will eventually become a lead.

The second mailer is much more targeted. The second mailer that we're going to talk about later in this book briefly and is a lead nurture mailer. This mailer is sent to prospects who have previously raised their hand to get something from you. And you can also send that mailer to your sphere of influence (SOI) in order to remain in front of them once a month consistently. I don't know about you, but I gladly spent 68 cents/month on my past clients to remain in front of them. And remember, people open the mail when they are the least distracted.

For access to all the free Resources and Trainings mentioned in this book, please go to:

www.MailerMomResources.com

CHAPTER 2

MAILERS FOR LEAD GENERATION

FIVE SUCCESS KEYS FOR YOUR MAILER

> *"Success is not the key to happiness. Happiness is the key to success. If you love what you're doing, you will be successful!"*
> - Albert Schweitzer

Every mailer has five components that I want you to think about when you create it.

1. **Action**: What's in it for the prospect
2. **Audience**: Who is it for?
3. **Attention**: What will gain their attention in a creative (imagery)?
4. **Advertisement**: What will gain their attention in a creative (text)?
5. **Activation**: What will happen after the prospect becomes a lead?

1. ACTION

We're actually starting with the most important component, the action. What is the action that you want them to take when they receive your mail piece? I like to refer to them as a value item. What are you going to offer them of value that would make them become a lead? We really want to start thinking with the end in mind. What's your call to action, for short CTA, going to be? Most agents have a very basic call to action on their mailer. Call me. I urge you in today's day and age to get away from the only call to action being: 'Call me!'.

And I will explain to you why. Sending a piece of mail will cost you money. What is your ultimate goal when you send the mailer? Your ultimate goal to send the mailer is to generate a lead. What is a lead? A lead is considered a name and some way to contact them such as their email, address or phone number. I often revert to emails simply because I'm not a caller and it just doesn't fit into my marketing model, trying to make a phone call while I have my toddler throwing a tantrum that he cannot have the fifth piece of chocolate.

But if you are a caller or you have a calling department or an inside sales associate (ISA), and that's your preferred form, you can simply switch your call to action to something that will generate phone numbers as opposed to emails. But more on that later.

So the very first thing that I suggest everybody does is to make sure they have a solid call to action. The #1 action item a real estate agent can offer is a free or complimentary home evaluation report or CMA. I'm still surprised to see how many agents do not have an instant home valuation website. Why instant? It's really simple. We want instant gratification at all times. Think about your television experience. Are you still watching television shows with commercial interruptions? Or are you able to skip commercials with the push of a button? Maybe you are watching without any commercials at all?? If so, think further. Why is this important? It gives the end consumer the option to not delay their viewing experience. Instant gratification.

The life we live is a very on demand life. I used to look forward to the commercial breaks because this meant I was able to go to the bathroom and refill my drink as well as get a snack. Now, my kids simply pause their show and do things whenever they feel the need to. Things really have changed. And it's just important that we change as well. So I'm going to leave you with a few suggestions for automatic home evaluation sites that will not break the bank.

CLOUD CMA

The first one is Cloud CMA. Cloud CMA is an amazing tool that you can use across the US to generate seller leads. And here's how it works: A prospect will go to a landing page, on which they can enter their address. The system tells them they found the address and have a value report ready.It then asks the prospect where they would like to receive this report. The lead enters their email address and submits their information.You will receive an email notification for a new lead and because it is something that the prospect really wants (as opposed to a forced open house invite or a neighborhood newsletter) you will most often receive a valid email address. Really cool, right?

Now here is where most people are saying, "But those reports are not accurate. This is nothing better than the Zestimate." And yes, it is not going to be as good as you doing your job. And what is your job? Your job is to connect with people in order to help them the best. And how can you do this? By connecting with them and then servicing them to the point where they will have a good experience. A free report cannot and will not replace you, but it will open the door for you to have a conversation with a lead.

Listings 2 Leads

The second tool I want to share with you is Listings To Leads. Listings To Leads also lets you generate landing pages for your listings in order to capture someone's attention and generate a lead. The service starts at $40/month at the time of writing this book and is in my opinion a great contender for agents to enter the world of online lead generation in the most simplistic way possible.

They have tools for **Buyer Lead Generation** such as:

- Buyer Leads: Down Payment Assistance Programs
- Buyer Leads: Countdown Clock
- Buyer Leads: VIDEO: Home Improvements
- Buyer Leads: Loan Programs

They have tools for **Seller Lead Generation** such as:

- Seller Leads: Valuation Landing Page
- Seller Leads: Nearby Sold Homes
- Seller Leads: Selling Agent
- Seller Leads: Just Sold General
- Seller Leads: Just Sold Specific Listing
- Seller Leads: Pending General Area
- Seller Leads: Pending Specific Listing
- Seller Leads: Just Listed Specific Listing
- Seller Leads: Selling Under 30 Days

- Seller Leads: Empty Nester
- Seller Leads: Sold in 7 Days
- Seller Leads: FSBO
- Seller Leads: Expired Listings

Remember though before you get swooped up in the glitzy shiny world of possibilities that it is essential to have a plan in place. Otherwise you will get overwhelmed wanting to implement it all and are ending with nothing, leaving you feeling defeated and frustrated! Solid strategy first, find the matching tactics secondary!

HOMEBOT

The third tool I want to share with you is Homebot. Homebot, I personally do not have much experience with, however, based on some research for this book, they have a lot of features that stood out and made it on the list worth checking out. The homebot service starts at $25/month at the time of writing this book and they have finally put out a lead capture feature as well! One of the things to note on their system: The potential lead will enter their address and receive a value number right off the bat. Then they are asked if they would want the full report sent via email. This might work out great potentially to attract thorough people, but it might also backfire and lead to a higher site rate, leaving you without a lead and a lot of freebie seekers.. How would you know? The only way to find out is through testing.

Just to be clear I have no affiliations with any of these, but I do think that having an automated home evaluation tool in your real estate marketing box is absolutely crucial for your real estate success in today's day and age!

> *PRO TIP:*
>
> *Don't want to pay for a tool like this? Check with your brokerage or local MLS if they are providing you something like this as part of their services.*

3. AUDIENCE

Next up, we want to think about audiences. Who is going to receive our mailers? Is this going to be for the HGTV-loving person that thinks she knows it all because she's been watching HGTV for the last six months? "HGTV-approved design hacks to give you more money when you sell!" might be a great way to get this person's attention! In general, you want to be very clear on who you're trying to target. Have you ever heard the statement: 'Jack of all trades, master of none". You cannot target everybody. Most agents fail because of this simple principle. What do I mean by this? You cannot target 20-year-olds that have never owned a home with the same language you would use to target 60-year olds moving out of their big home in order to downsize. So let's go through some of the basics on how to find your ideal customer's language. This following principle has been something that I picked up from an amazing copywriter named Jim Edwards, on how to connect with your ideal client. He refers to this person as F.R.E.D.

F.R.E.D. stands for Fear, Results, Expectations, Desire.

> *You want to think about your customer. What do THEY think they need? This is the most important principle where most real estate agents and business owners take a completely wrong turn and after reading this section in this book, it will change the way you approach your marketing message and help you level up your business. Ask yourself these 4 questions when creating your marketing message:*

1. What are their problems?
2. What are their questions?
3. What are their roadblocks?
4. What are the results they want?

Let's put this into a short example!

WHO:

You want to target home sellers that are looking to upsize.

Their problem:

They need to sell their current home.

Their questions:

When is the perfect time to start looking for a home? Do we buy a home first? Will they accept our offer if we haven't listed our home yet? Can we finance both homes?

Roadblocks:

Now we are taking it one step further. What stands in their way? What do they have to overcome? Let's think about their lives. Chances are they are busy with their children and work and their time is limited. They try to research their problems but end up with contradicting information leaving them feeling even more confused than before.

Results:

What is it that they are really looking for? A clear cut way that shows them how to sell their home with the least hassle and positions them in the right spot to purchase their dream home that has enough room to fit everyone in their family.

As you can see, language is important, and you need to be aware of who you're talking to at all times.

3. ATTENTION

What's an eye-catching image? What images stand out? This is where I want to talk about how to create a captivating image or a creative hook, in short something that draws their eyes and catches their attention. And this is where I'm going to insert a little soapbox speech, why I think most of the mailing companies out there are just having lower conversion rates. Most of them are junk, excuse my bluntness. They are meant to appeal to the masses for real estate agents, but they really don't appeal to the masses of consumers. A consumer doesn't want to feel like this is just another piece of mail sent to them.

A mailer should be fully customizable to you and your brand. Most of the mailers are not very catchy when it comes to standing out from the pile of advertisements that are getting sent to somebody's mailbox.

But what is going to grab somebody's attention? And this really depends on who you are targeting. Are you targeting retirees in 55+ communities as your niche? Do you think a picture of a family is going to stand out or a picture of an older couple, looking at a sunset? Whatever you think is their vision or their happy place, that's a really good way to start thinking about a design that will match your ideal lead.

What if you're targeting somebody as a move up buyer? Their house has gotten too small. Kids toys are everywhere. They're trying to entertain, work and live life. Hit on their pain point. Remember our list of the top 10 reasons people take actions? #5: Move away from mental or physical pain and #6 Get more comfort. Those are just a few examples of how you can see why some things work and other mailers fall flat.

And when it comes to a captivating image and headline, I do suggest that you refer back to the framework of 10 reasons people take actions and make sure that your postcard is targeting at least two of the pillars why somebody should take action, if not more.

I want to give you a few more tips on how to make sure your mailers are captivating for your ideal target audience.

SIZE

First up, odd sizes are definitely something that can stand out in the mail. If you send an elongated mailer as opposed to everything else is rectangular, or even if you send a square one, you might stand out from the pile.

BRIGHT COLORS

The mailer should also be pretty bright and colorful. We want it to really stand out and grab attention. Yellow for example has been proven to be a very successful color. This is one of the reasons wholesalers and investors are reverting back to the little yellow letter or sticky note strategy.

IMAGES

I suggest you do not use boring stock images that are screaming run-of-the-mill mailers that are sent to thousands of people with the push of one button. Sometimes what works pretty well is real images that make the mailer look more intriguing to the prospect. Would you double look at a mailer that actually looks like a regular picture? I sure would. Here's one that might go a little bit against the grain. A mailer image on the front does not have to correlate to your message. It doesn't have to be relevant at all. Sounds crazy, but think about the Geico lizard. The Geico lizard is now a simple icon standing for the company. Having an animal on there for insurance doesn't really make any sense at all. You could also send mailers with dogs or cats on it consistently if you want to market to dog lovers or cat people. They will definitely take note of your mailer

4. Advertisement framework

What's the story? How is it relevant to your prospect? And this part, it's probably one of the most crucial. This is where you get to build a connection with your lead. This is where you want your prospect to start shaking or nodding their head to agree with you. You want to make sure that they can align with what you have to offer.

An emotional connection is very helpful on a mailer. Most people approach prospects on a very businesslike level still however. And then they wonder why their mailer doesn't convert. A prospect does not want to be approached in a businesslike manner. They do not care that you have sold millions in that subdivision, because it's not valuable to them. You want to make sure that they see the value in using your services for themselves based on their perceived value of you. There are many instances where I sit down with a prospect and their reason for hiring me is not because I sold their neighbors home but because I am giving back to the community. Once I started noticing that, I had some more food for thought which translated into a better story to connect with my ideal prospect on a more meaningful level.

So what is the advertisement framework I use that has prospects read it and think: "Oh my gosh, I need it"?

HEADLINE

The first thing you want to have in your advertising framework is a captivating headline. Something that grabs their attention and makes them want to read the rest.

EMOTIONAL CONNECTION

After the headline, you have a small emotional story. For example, "This is how the seller walked away with $20,000 more in their pocket and they couldn't be happier."

BRIDGE

Then the next part is what we call a bridge. This is where we want to paint the dream picture. Anybody ever been on Instagram and wondered why some accounts have so many followers? Well, if you actually look at their pictures, most of them are dream pictures where people are posting what they would love their life to look like. Instagram is a very dream-focused platform, and that's what we want to do with this bridge. We want to showcase to them, what can life be like after you hire us as your agent, getting results like these? For example, if we continue on with our happy seller: *"Now he can finally enjoy the boating life he's always dreamed of."*

MECHANISM

Now that we've painted the picture of the outcome, let's show them how we did it. What's the mechanism that gave our seller that outcome? *"If you want to be as happy as this seller, we want to share with you our five-step process when listing a home."*

CALL TO ACTION

A call to action is giving your prospect an action to do, such as schedule a call, register, download, claim, sign up, etc. This is how they know what to do next. Are you sending them to a website? Do they need to get on your schedule?

Do you expect them to register for something? You want to let them know, actually you want to spell it out for them: What's the next step?

> *PRO TIP:*
>
> *You can use this advertisement framework on anything! Flyers, social media, Online Ads on Facebook, Google PPC and more! The universal framework works on them all!*

5. ACTIVATION

The fifth success key is activation. What happens once they raise their hand and say, "I want to take action. I want to get the value item you were talking about"? What does your online path for your lead look like? What is your follow up process? And this is where the magic happens. There's a reason that somebody said and coined the phrase, "The fortune is in the follow-up." It is rare that we are completing a transaction based on somebody raising their hand for the first time. Let's compare it to dating. The first date is where we put our feelers out to check out the other person. Most often if everything looks good, a second date follows. The dating continues until someone pops the questions and then there might be children and joined pets and other assets.

Just like dating, real estate is a relationship building business. This is the part where too many people are getting swooped up in sales. And instead of focusing on building a relationship, getting to know the person, and having the person get to know them, they are focusing on giving them houses to look at and all the other things that we are told to do. Imagine that your date was going to go down on one knee asking you if you wanted to get married and have two beautiful children and live in a home in the suburbs on the first day you met. You probably would have looked at your date like they are crazy and never, ever talked to that person again.

So let's start by focusing on the relationship that we have with that lead. If you raised your hand and came into my world for the first time, what impression would I want to make on you? I probably first want you to get to know me a little bit better. And I also want you to like me.

Because remember, I can't just ask you for all your trust upfront, such as, "Hey, let me see your pre-approval before I even send you any houses." Yet, that's what most agents do and then they wonder why their leads are not converting. I want to be very honest here. If somebody asks me for my bank statement without even saying, "Hello, how are you? Here are my credentials." I probably do not want to get into a conversation with them about my finances. I do think it's very important for us to know what they can truly afford, but this right now is not the time for this conversation.

Just like dating, you want to build a relationship with the prospect, show them that you are in the marketplace successfully buying and selling real estate, showcasing your clients, your clients testimonials, offering them guidance along the way before you are able to go and sit down at the table with them to have this serious talk. What's the easiest way for you to figure out what the path should be once a prospect comes into your world? How about you simply put yourself into your lead's shoes.

Assume for a little bit that you are a seller thinking about selling and you finally were brave enough to push that little button online that says request a free CMA. What would you want your path to look like?

Would you want somebody starting to call you immediately saying, "Hey, thanks so much. When can I come out and see you?" If this is a yes and this is your personality, that's fine. If this is a no, what else would you have liked to happen instead? Maybe a welcome package delivered to the doorstep? Maybe a personal note card sent into your mailbox. The options are endless. And the nice thing about our business is the fact that you can customize it and make it 1000% something that you are envisioning. Don't limit yourself to what you think it should be, but make sure that you can fully stand behind the system that you are creating. Which brings me to my final point:

Activation is all about the mindset behind marathon versus sprint. I would love to finish running my mile as quickly as possible. Sprint, sprint, sprint, sprint, sprint. However, not only is it going to lead to a burnout, chances are I will never ever make the mile in a sprint. Our business should be viewed as a marathon. Every day we're pushing forward just a little bit more. Finding our perfect pipeline filled with customers is essential for us to establish a healthy business with a marathon mindset. Think about your pipeline customer like your water reservoir. You will always need to have something in your pipeline in order to keep going.

If our water reservoir in our marathon is depleted, we will run out of steam and eventually stop. This result of it, an income roller coaster. So while sprints and quick transactions are great, they're also not sustainable as they don't happen frequently enough for our business to thrive. So if your business is here to remain for the long run, I want you to really consider pipelines as your lifeline, your water tank, your reservoir to make it to the finish line.

One of the ways I add quick wins for my team is with rental leads. Rental leads are the sprint transaction. They are quick, they are fast and they typically can close anywhere from 1-2 weeks to 30 to 60 days. So here's your question. Are you in it for a marathon or are you in it for the sprint? It's your turn to decide how you want to build your business.

LEAD GENERATION MAILERS

> *"Give a man a fish and you feed him for a day, teach a man to fish and you will feed him for a lifetime!"* - Chinese proverb

Now that we discussed all the components for lead generation, it's time to put the pieces together. The Lead Generation Mailers are mainly used to identify a potential lead from a cold audience and get them to raise their hand. This way they are self-identifying themselves and you can work on nurturing the lead into a client with a follow up sequence that warms them up and moves them into the warm and hot audience category. At the same time this step helps to justify spending a bit more money on that potential client for lead nurture.

For example:

If you are sending high-gloss tri-fold large brochures to an entire neighborhood you are looking at over $2/brochure/household. Most of these people are not looking to transact at this very moment.

So instead, you are sending them a mailer at a lower cost and only send that brochure to people after they have raised their hand. This will not only increase your touches with the potential prospect but also allow you to increase your area without increasing your marketing budget. There are two ways you can go about identifying a cold audience and we are going to go over these next.

THE BLANKET

> *"Today I will do what others won't! So tomorrow I can do what others can't!"* - Jerry Rice

The first approach works like a blanket and is covering a large area at the lowest cost possible. I personally think this is one of the best approaches for cold audiences because it is easy on the wallet. This works extremely well for geographic farming as you are able to build brand awareness in the process. Not everyone living in that area will be matching your marketing message and therefore your mailer won't resonate with them (remember the difference between speaking to a seller vs speaking to a buyer)

So, let's dive into the anatomy of the lead gen mailer for brand awareness. The lead gen mailer for brand awareness is more of a blanket-style approach. You are sending that mailer to a cold audience, to people who don't know you. And I suggest you are using a service that makes this highly affordable. One of the ways we could do that is through a service called Every Door Direct Mail or short EDDM, a service provided by the United States Postal Service

(USPS). This service allows you to send mailers for 18 cents in postage. It does not get much cheaper than this.

The printing costs for one mail piece is typically around 18 cents as well, which will bring your total mail piece costs printed and delivered to 36 cents/mailer. As you can see, this is by far one of the most cost-effective ways to send a blanket-style mailing out for you to generate leads. Again, this needs to be into an area where there is a high enough turnover rate to sustain your business goals. Just a reminder that we have an entire resource section for you loaded with items such as my Profitable Geographic Farming Cheat Sheet to download. This will help you determine if your area is indeed a 'profitable farm'. Every Door Direct Mail is done by postal routes, which means that you have no way of selecting the individual homes that you want to target as it will simply go by a predetermined route that the postman delivers to each day.

You can't do a partial route mailing either and the balance needs to be paid in full online or at the post office when dropping off these mailings. For more details on EDDM Mailings along with sizing for them, you can find further details in the resource section of this book.

If the blanket-approach is what you have selected, it's time to put the other pieces in place. Who are you going to target? What are their problems? What solution can you offer them? What action do they have to take?

BULLSEYE-TARGETING

"And Archer cannot hit the bulls-eye, if he doesn't know where the target is!" - anonymous

The second option to reach a cold audience is by sending targeted mailers. This means you are being selective who receives your mail. I just recently launched a campaign for an agent based on a demographic feature of length of ownership. The assumption is that if they have owned their home for more than 20+ years they are likely going to sell sooner than other owners in that target area

Our mailer results are coming in as I am writing this book and the response rate has been phenomenal. Each mailing of $280 procured 1 appointment (and we are only on mailing #2 with an expected snowball effect to happen within the next few short months ahead). The price points for the listings are coming to a sum of over $12,000 in commission for the listing agent side. Now the question for you: Would you spend $560 to make $12,000? So even after you deduct the cost of the mailers you are looking at a 21x return on your money! WOWZA!

While the bullseye-targeting method is a lot more expensive, it is also much more targeted which means you can tailor your marketing message much more effectively. And if you are zooming in on something, well, the results get dialed in as well. So while your investment might be higher, you are also able to get a higher return on your investment. Now that we looked at these two different approaches, let's go one level deeper.

3 WAYS TO USE TARGETING FOR LEAD GENERATION

"A river cuts through rock, not because of its strength but its persistence!" - Jim Watkins

GEOGRAPHIC TARGETING

The first one I want to highlight is geographic farming. Geographic farming is when you are concentrating your mailing efforts into a specific local area. Most agents make the mistake and just try and figure out if the area that they're selecting is good because they live in it. Well, this could not be a worst idea. What you actually want to make sure of is the fact that the geographic area you're selecting is a profitable farm. A profitable farm has enough business happening to sustain your income goals. For a complete guide on geographic farming, you can download my free Geographic Farming Cheat Sheet that you can find in the Resource Section of this book. You can also send targeted Mailers into a geographic farm. For example, could you focus on becoming the #1 agent in a specific town and have your mail pieces only go into the geographic area of that town based on the niche or demographic you are targeting. Almost like a hybrid model if you want between geographic targeting and our next two categories.

DEMOGRAPHIC TARGETING

The second thing we could target is based on people, demographic targeting. What if you only wanted to target home owners that have owned their house for at least 20 years? Why would you want to do that? Well, we will talk in the next few chapters about making sure your language matches who you're trying to gain as an ideal lead. Building a relationship with them over mail can be a beneficial way for you to do more business. Or what if you wanted to target renters? You could target renters in order to build up your first time buyer arsenal. How do you know if somebody's a renter? There are services out there that you can utilize, or you could simply build your mailing list by checking your MLS for rental properties that have previously been advertised for rent.

Also, a great way to look for rentals is by filtering for properties that are held in an LLC, as many management companies will do this. You can also send mailers to apartment com plex sand of course, you can target anything in between. Maybe you are looking for people to upsize or people who have been homeowners for at least five years. Again, there is no wrong answer of what is the most profitable as long as you do it the right way and follow the steps of a successful mailer I previously outlined

Niche marketing

The third way you can target people with your postcard mailers is by property characteristics. Maybe you want to become known in one specific building. You could simply mail that specific building. Or maybe you want to do ocean front properties. Let's be honest, who doesn't want to have a place with a view?

Maybe your niche is specializing in penthouse condos, or you want to only target three bedroom town homes because you know everybody is looking to upsize into a three bedroom from a two bedroom, or you know people like to downsize from their house into a three bedroom? Maybe you want to target homes built at a specific period in time. I actually have an agent in my area that specializes in homes that are considered mid century modern. So you'll see when you ask, "What is the most profitable way to send postcards? Who should you send it to?" The answer is, it depends. And it depends most on what you want your business to look like. I also want to make sure you check out the resource section as I have added my free PDF on 50 Real Estate Niches to choose from along with a complimentary 10-minute training video for you to check out!

MY TOP 10 SELLER MAILERS - GET MORE LEADS AND MORE LISTINGS

> *"Don't wait until you achieve your goal to be proud of yourself! Be proud of every step you take towards reaching your goal!"* - unknown

If you are anything like me you appreciate a good book that is not just theory, but also real examples that can help you start thinking in the right direction. So I wanted to include for you my TOP 10 Seller Mailers.

I HAVE A BUYER MAILER

You could send an I-have-a-client postcard mailer. You might know about the letter version of it, but what if we just put it out there in postcard format? Obviously, don't lie. Make sure that you actually have somebody looking with the general criteria, but you can definitely send out an I-have-a-client postcard mailer to get people to raise their hand and say, "Hey, we've been thinking about selling. What exactly is your client looking for? If they are a great fit, perfect. You might even have a double-sided deal. If they are not a perfect fit, maybe you end up with a new listing.

NEIGHBORHOOD STATISTICS

Neighborhood statistics are another great mailer to send because many times people are not quite sure where their home value falls in. So seeing a neighborhood statistic and a range might actually give them enough encouragement to place a phone call or request their own CMA. I have had people who've been very surprised on how high their home can potentially sell for. I've also had people being disappointed that the market wasn't quite there where they were hoping it was. Getting somebody to raise their hand is the first step we need to do in order for us to help them.

HOME VALUATION

Home evaluation mailers are probably the #1 offer that we as real estate agents have available. It's really important to make sure we have a captivating image that does not look like one of those generic postcard mailer websites, because they could look spammy and not trustworthy. Remember to refer back to my suggestions on a few services for instant home valuation tools earlier in this book.

FREE REPORT/VALUE ITEM

This mailer is one of my favorite ones. I get to provide value to my prospects by simply giving them the opportunity to learn more with my value item. These can be simple things such as a free staging guide, a short webinar, a case study of how I sold their neighbor's house for $20,000 more, or anything else that you can potentially consider relevant for your ideal prospect.

JUST LISTED MAILER

The next mailer is a just-listed mailer. Just-listed mailers are by far the most commonly used mailers. Remember when I said that most agents think about their mailers as a marketing piece for their listing as opposed to a lead generation tool? A just-listed mailer does not need the property description on it. A just-listed mailer can drive curiosity for the neighbors to figure out what happened to their home value now that the neighbors have listed their home.

JUST SOLD MAILER

The second most utilized mailer is a just-sold mailer. Now, this one is not for marketing the property anymore for most agents. However, it is a mailer that many agents send with a very weak call to action. Can you guess what it is? You guessed it: Call/Contact me! Remember, we talked about the fact that mailer objectives can go from easy to hard? You want to make sure that you have the lowest barrier of entry when it comes to your mailers in order to maximize your return on your investment or ROI.

So what should be on a great just-sold mailer? What is the first thing that changes with a new closed property? The neighborhood home value has been impacted. This is something that a potential future seller may want to keep tabs on. So why not let them know their home value changed and they can have an updated home value report simply by going to your website. You could also say something along the lines of:

> "We've done it. Our seller got the highest price possible for his property and the way we did it was through our five-step marketing plan. That's right, five steps that are having a massive impact on your neighbors' bottom line. Want to download the five steps?? Simply go here."

This is an easy way for them to see behind the scene where you can showcase your expertise on a subject matter.

UNDER CONTRACT MAILER

I really have not seen too many people use under-contract mailer. I have to admit it's really tricky to know when to send them because you don't want to send them too early and have the property get reactivated. And you don't want to send them too late when the property is already closed, because you will be sending a just-closed mailer.

I will also say that I do not send under-contract mailers for my buyer purchases. However, if you wanted to, you definitely could. The under-contract mailer I personally send in order to increase my touches and interactions with the surrounding neighbors. I use it as another form of social proof in which I let them know that I was hired to sell their property and I'm proud to report that this is now under contract. I can also share a few things with them, such as, "I have another 20 buyers that were interested, but the home was not quite right. If you are looking to sell, give me a call or go to this website, or send me an email, or claim your Smart Seller report." I want to make sure I utilize this opportunity to generate more leads for my business.

COMING SOON MAILER

This one I had to include because it is acceptable where I'm at to do coming-soon marketing. I know some of you may have picked up this book in different states with different restrictions. Coming-soon marketing is something that you need to figure out if it is allowed where you are located. You know how that saying goes: When in doubt, talk to your managing broker. However, coming-soon marketing can be especially beneficial to gain additional insights from people. The response rate on it is amazing.

With coming-soon marketing, you can take advantage of curious buyers and future sellers. You can take advantage of people knowing people to potentially work both sides of the deal or refer a potential buyer out to somebody else and get a referral fee. It also showcases your willingness to do things differently than the average agent, which makes you stand out from the crowd and help you gain more listing and buying opportunities.

UVP MAILER

UVP stands for unique value proposition. Let me give you a few examples. Coldwell Banker stands for one of the oldest brokerages since the 1800's leading people home and their brand color blue represents the trust factor as well. Redfin's UVP is a 1% listing fee if you buy or sell with them. iBuyers are betting heavily that many homeowners are willing to trade the top-dollar of an open market listing for the certainty of a cash offer in hand and their value proposition is speed, certainty, and simplicity. And the list goes on.

Do you have a unique value proposition? A lot of the real estate agents back in the day during the housing crisis had to become very creative when it came time to buy and sell property. So many times, we saw guarantees in real estate that can be helpful to set you apart from the competition. For example, an agent in my area accompanies every single showing of his listing. This is his unique value proposition. I also know agents that are giving a home purchase guarantee. All of these things are making that real estate agent unique from all the other agents. What is your unique selling point?

TESTIMONIAL & FUNNY MAILERS

A testimonial mailer is simply stating that you are capable of getting the job done. You have a review from a person that you are showcasing, which creates social proof and gives the potential lead the feeling of security that you know what you're doing and you are an expert in your field.

A funny mailer is something where you also can highlight the fact that you know what you're doing. I personally use this one on my pre-listing packages, which is a cute little image of a couple sitting at the table. The husband is reading the paper, the below caption states, "Oh, look, this agent sold the little house made out of straw for $500,000. This is the agent we should use." A little bit of humor can go a long way to connect with your ideal prospect and generate more leads and more listings.

THEORIES FOR JUST LISTED/JUST SOLD/UNDER CONTRACT/COMING SOON MAILERS

> *"It's not about selling. It's about creating value for your audience!"*
> *- Jerry Allocca*

Did you know that there are actually two theories out there of where you should send just listed and just sold mailers? Let me share these with you:

THEORY #1

Theory #1 is stating that you should send Just Listed and Just Sold mailers to a radius surrounding the property. You will have the highest relevance score surrounding the property. People want to know what is happening in their neighborhood. They are much more likely to opt in to your offer because their home value is directly tied to and impacted by the neighbor's price point. People also recognize the style of home as a home in their neighborhood and some might even recognize the street name to tie the property back into their own neighborhood.

THEORY #2

Theory #2 is based on establishing social proof in your geographic farm or with your sphere of influence. In that theory, you would take the just-listed and just sold mailers and mail it into your geographic farm for proof that you are successful doing business or send it to your database if this is how you choose to grow your business. By doing so you are increasing the amount of touches you are having with your database throughout the year to stay in front of them and remind them that you are in business to help people with their real estate needs.

For access to all the free Resources and Trainings mentioned in this book, please go to:

www.MailerMomResources.com

CHAPTER 3

MAILERS FOR LEAD NURTURE

THE FORTUNE IS IN THE FOLLOW-UP

> *"Believe you can and you're halfway there!"* - Theodore Roosevelt

The second type of mailer is a lead nurture mailer. But that's not all this mailer can do! This type of mailer is also great for your very own sphere of influence. This mailer can be sent out monthly to a targeted list. The cost for a targeted mailer is a bit higher than the blanket approach. And it should run you about 68 cents/piece.

The purpose of the mailer is simple. Stay in front of your sphere of influence to stay top of mind. It also helps to stay in front of the leads that have previously raised their hand, so you can nurture the relationship and convert them into a client.

While the cost for this list is higher, the list is also going to be smaller.

As mentioned above, this is one of the best ways to make sure you remain in front of your sphere during the time they are the least distracted, when opening the mail. Personally I like to have these mailers branded with my avatar as well. And this is not because I am vain but because it has been proven that people remember faces better than names. I want my clients to remember who their agent was when they sold or bought a house with me three, five or fifteen years ago. One of my favorite ways to do this is by using a full body image of myself with a clear background. This is not my professional headshot but still a professional image. Think about it like your mini cardboard cutout visiting their mailbox every month. A great website to use for this that is free is www.remove.bg

Here are some examples of lead nurture mailers by each quarter of the year for inspiration! There are enough examples in there to pick and choose or build a campaign out of the following suggestions for 2 years!

Quarter 1: JANUARY/FEBRUARY/MARCH

- What's my home worth?
- Market Review/Market Predictions
- A Unique Value Proposition
- Comparison: Rent VS Buy
- Get Spring Market Ready
- Paint Guide/Color Trends

Quarter 2: APRIL/MAY/JUNE

- Local Farmers Markets
- Running Event Calendar
- Baseball Schedule
- Local (Music) Festivals
- Local Attractions Guide
- Environmental hacks for your home

Quarter 3: JULY/AUGUST/SEPTEMBER

- 4th of July Fireworks
- Football Schedule
- Event Guide
- Back to School
- Shop Local/Vendor Highlights
- The Great Outdoors: Trails & Hikes

Quarter 4: OCTOBER/NOVEMBER/DECEMBER

- Apple Orchards
- Pumpkin Patches & Corn Mazes
- Fall Maintenance Schedule
- Thankful & Giving Back

- Ice Skating Rinks
- Local Theatres Guide

SUCCESS STORY NURTURE

Another approach to Nurture Mailers are Success Stories! And when I say success stories, I do not talk about you saying you Sold yet another home! Success Stories are the stories behind a transaction:

Stories such as:

- The 1st time home buyer that was scared to make the jump but trusted you! After months of getting their credit affairs in order, enough credit was established to purchase the very first home without a cosigner.
- The couple that you helped sell their home facing the expressway to get a home on a cul de sac so their kids can ride their bicycles without the parents constant fear of accidents.
- The widow that was sitting alone in a home that was empty and too big and finally made the decision to say goodbye to the home that her children grew up in, in order to move to a flourishing 55+ community where she is now president of the gardening club and enjoys time with people that share her interest

The stories are endless. Select 12 of them and focus on the win that was achieved through trusting you (the mechanism). By sharing stories on your lead nurture mailers, people can see your success and at the same time find the story they associate with the most! Not sure where to start? Go through your testimonials if you have some. These make for great beginnings of your success stories.

For access to all the free Resources and Trainings mentioned in this book, please go to:

www.MailerMomResources.com

CHAPTER 4

THE NERDY CHAPTER

DIRECT MAIL STATISTICS FOR 2021

Welcome to the nerdy chapter. This one is for all my number wizards out there. Did you know that the response rate in 2020 was 4.9% for targeted lists? All right, all things aside, we know 2020 was a little bit of a crazy year. Your average mailer response rate is 1-2%, but let me give you 12 other facts about direct mail that will probably blow your mind.

1. Direct mail spend—at **$38.5 billion**—accounts for the largest portion of US local advertising spend.
2. US advertisers spend an average of **$167** per person on direct mail.
3. These US advertisers also earn an average **$2,095** worth of goods sold through direct mail per person.
4. **70%** of consumers say direct mail is more personal than online interactions.
5. **54%** of consumers say they want direct mail from brands that interest them.
6. Direct mail open rates can reach up to **90%**.
7. **42%** of recipients read or scan the direct mail they receive.
8. Direct mail response rates are 5-9x higher than any other advertising channel.

9. The average direct mail response rate for prospect lists was **4.9%** last year (2020).
10. Adding a name to your direct mail piece can increase response rates by **135%**.
11. **62%** of consumers who responded to direct mail in the past three months made a purchase.
12. **39%** of consumers try a business for the first time because of direct mail.

Stats provided courtesy of Nerdwallet:

https://www.fundera.com/resources/direct-mail-statistics

SIZE OF POSTCARD MAILERS

Let's start with postcard sizes. This one has so many people wondering, what is the perfect size to send mailers? Is it a small one? Is it a half a sheet of paper? Is it a full size one? One of the jumbo mailers? Postcards come in all shapes and sizes, so let's go over some of the most commonly used ones and when you might consider using them. Of course, there are sizes in between. Elongated ones, taller ones that you often see with menus for restaurants. Honestly, they all work. But for the sake of this book, we're going to be simply categorizing it into these three main mailing sizes, small, medium, and large.

You might still be wondering, what is the exact size that people actually use for these mailers? We have included a few of the most commonly used mailing sizes in the resource chapter of this book for you and included bleed and printing parameters so you can find out what the ideal size is when it comes to the design.

SMALL POSTCARD

The most cost-effective one to send is definitely our small 6 x 4 postcard mailer. This is the size of a postcard and by far the most cost-effective one. It is also the one that most often gets lost in the pile of junk mail, so you may want to save a few dollars, but the effectiveness offered is questionable.

However I'm not saying they don't work. Because all mailers work, but it's definitely harder to grab somebody's attention if you are stuck in the giant pile of advertisements that are just overshadowing this small postcard. When might you be using this postcard? I generally would suggest you try and use this postcard when you are starting out and have a smaller budget.

Because of its size, I also think this postcard, if you can time the delivery of it, should not be delivered with your weekly grocery ads, because it will likely go under with all the colorful sendouts from the grocery stores that arrive in the mailbox.

MEDIUM POSTCARD

The next common size is a 6 x 9. A 6 x 9 is a pretty decent size for the fact that it is larger and most often printed on heavier cardstock with a glossy finish. This is definitely a piece that will grab attention in your mail. It is still fairly cost-effective, yet also gets the message across pretty well. You have a lot of advertisement space, which personally I love, because it gives you enough room to potentially co-brand your mailers. Images are easy to see, and you can appeal to folks who don't want to get their reading glasses out when looking at a piece of mail.

LARGE POSTCARD MAILER

Then there is the jumbo mailer. The jumbo mailer is essentially a full-size sheet of paper, which definitely stands out in your mailbox. Many people will examine this one a little bit closer because it is one of the less commonly used mail sizes, and with anything, if something is less commonly used, less widely spread, people are curious what it is and will take the time to check it out.

PRINTING GUIDE

Printing seems to be something that many people have questions on regularly. Where do you get your mailers printed? How much is it to get postcards printed? And I want to make sure that you had a chapter in this book to reference when the time came for you to select a printer. First things first, how much is it going to be? And the short answer, it depends. We covered two different styles of postcard mailings in this book. One is a more blanket-like approach with a service called Every Door Direct Mail with the United States postal service. Sizing will make a difference for price as well. The blanket approach will be by far the cheapest option to send mail. The cost to print the mail pieces as it is a bulk printing is typically about 18 cents a piece for a small or medium sized mailer. And the postage comes out to about 18 cents a piece as well, giving you a total of 36 cents per address on the midsize tier.

The other approach is a more targeted style in which you are selecting only certain addresses. This one is definitely more expensive and runs about 68 cents per address. Remember, these are just guidelines based on my own mailings and your actual costs might vary slightly. However, you should be in the general ballpark of these numbers. What I do want to help you with is finding a more cost-effective way of printing.

Xpressdocs

The first option I'm going to suggest is one that is widely available to everybody, which is xpressdocs.com. Again, I'm not affiliated with it; but I've used them personally with good results.

Xpressdocs.com lets you upload custom designs as well as lets you use their templates. Just as a reminder: I already talked to you guys about generic templates a little bit. Instead of using generic templates, I do suggest you are using mailers out of our Mailer Mom Library as they are fully customizable. But you can fully use this service to upload your complete design and send out your mailing.

Remine

The second alternative would be a service that is offered through a tax record software called Remine. Most of us in the U.S. have heard of Remine or have access to it as a reliable tax record resource. There is a mailing option associated with Remine that lets you upload a fully designed mailpiece. I have found however that their printing area is slightly off, leading to white spaces on the left and right side and the artwork/design will need adjustment. Also their quality is in my opinion not as good as the quality of printing companies. They do make it very easy to place your order as well and help generate targeted mailing lists with the click of a few buttons. So if you don't mind tweaking your mailers a bit, Remine might be a great choice!

Local Printing Company

The third option I'm going to suggest is by far the most local and cost-effective strategy I personally use. You have the option to find a local printing company, which will not only cut down the shipping costs, but they also might potentially be able to offer you a concierge service in which they will take care of bundling and dropping off your mailings to the post office for you for a small concierge fee.

This was definitely something that I was initially not taking advantage of because I was able to invest my own time as a resource and bundle and drop off all my mailings myself. However, the further my business grew, the more I loved having this as an option for ease of use and delivery. You can find local printing companies simply through a Google search or you can also utilize the resources at the United States Postal Service website and find approved EDDM vendors if you are looking for the blanket-style approach.

Vistaprint

I almost didn't include this one but shortly before giving this book over for production I ran a pricing quote comparison to see if Vistaprint would make the cut as a cost-effective alternative. And they did! Their mailing services are best used for targeted mailings. A great option if you are looking for a place to start sending your lead nurture mailers from!

You can upload your own list or purchase one from them. They have a complete design upload option as well as some real estate templates. I won't step back onto my soap box on some of the generic templates, just keep in mind that 'pretty' is not a postcard objective. Vistaprint does have some stand-out mail pieces you can use and draw inspiration from as well! Their printing quality is pretty good. You do only have two options at the moment for size (small and oversized) but this should be plenty to get you started. And my personal favorite: There is always an active coupon code for Vistaprint that you can use and apply! Give them a try!

THE RULES OF 1-1-1

We talked about images and text a lot in the last few chapters. I want to turn your attention to the contact form part. What should you include for your own contact information? I do think our postcards are an extension of our business cards, and therefore should have our professional headshot that is on most of our marketing material on the postcard. I also want to introduce you to the Rule of One. The Rule of One is based on how many forms of contact you should display. Should your office number be on there, or only your cell phone? The answer is, use the ONE number that will be the one where you are reachable for the majority of the time. In most instances, for real estate agents, that means the cell phone number. Use ONE email address, and display ONE website. By adding too many choices, you are simply confusing the lead with what action they should take. They have too many choices!

For example, when we are having a home valuation website displayed on our mailer, I suggest that you do not put in your personal real estate website on it as well, as these are now technically two links. Make sure you are pointing all arrows to the same place consistently. So when in doubt, follow the Rule of One for the most success. This way, you're also ensuring that the prospects that prefer the phone and who do not want to go on your website, can simply give you a call, and you are offering the prospects that do not enjoy phone conversation a simple way to connect with you via a website or email, just as efficiently.

THE RULE OF 7

Getting people to take action is getting harder and harder, mainly because we're so inundated with advertisements and sales messages that we are a lot more skeptical as humans. We are always on the lookout for: 'What's the catch?' I want to share with you the Marketing Rule of 7 that is fairly commonly known in the sales world. The rule of seven quite simply states that it takes an average of seven interactions with your brand before a purchase will take place.

When somebody has to interact with you at least seven times, how can you distribute this and make it happen? We are living in a day and age where it's not hard to have multiple channels. With mediums such as Facebook, Instagram, Twitter, email, mail, phone calls, text messages, TikToks and others, you'll have endless possibilities to be in front of your ideal target audience.

So what can this potentially look like for mail marketing? When you send a mailer, it is rarely the first mailer that gets interaction with the majority of prospects. Even though I have successfully helped agents send mailers where they have gotten a lead and an appointment out of the first mailer, for the majority of leads, it will take more than one mailer, especially if you are looking for consistent results. But once you send a mailer, this is one touch/interaction.

But you probably will not send a mailer a week later, so what can you do? One of the greatest things I suggest people do is being visible in the area with, for example, something like an open house. An open house in most instances is hosted by an agent with simply the brokerage sign up front. My friend, there is so much more potential an open house can give you. You can have your name on the open house sign. You can hand out invitations. You can have extra signs printed that you can distribute in the neighborhood to get people closer to the home, as well as see your name.

Once they are on your email list, they obviously should also see your email marketing. Is it time for another mailer? That would be touch number four already. Having social media advertisements in place can also help increase the interactions with your ideal prospect. Another great way to add touches to your ideal client is by knowing where they are spending their time on social media. Are there community groups for your neighborhood you can join? Are there district wide interest groups that you can be visible in? For example: Is there a local plant exchange Facebook Group for the Garden lover? Are there mom groups that allow parents to swap resources and meet new mom friends? Is it time for another mailer, and then another open house? You see, it does take a little bit of effort, but once you have a system in place of constantly being active and engaging with your potential lead, you will become a household name.

Did you notice, I did not say you have to be on all 15 social media platforms? The platform I encourage you to use to supplement any of your marketing efforts with mailers is the one that your prospect uses the most. Divide and conquer is much more effective than trying to do it all!

THE MATH BEHIND MAILERS

Let's dive into the math behind the mailers. What will make a mailer profitable? What are the numbers you should look at? I am going to list some of the most common formulas used for you next.

Cost per Mailpiece

Cost of Campaign ÷ Total # of Mailpieces= Cost per Mailpiece

Response Rate

of Responses ÷ # of Pieces Mailed x 100 = % Response Rate

Conversion Rate

Responses Resulting in Sales ÷ Total Responses x 100 = % Conversion Rate

Campaign Profit

Net Profit Resulting from Campaign - Campaign Expenses = Campaign Profits

Return on Investment (ROI)

Campaign Profits ÷ Campaign Expenses = % ROI

So now that you know the most important formulas, let's plug in some real numbers so you can see how it all works together.

Cost per Mailpiece

$300 ÷ 500 Mail Pieces = $0.60/mail piece

Response Rate

5 Responses ÷ 500 Pieces sent x 100 = 1%

Conversion Rate

2 Responses Resulting in Sales ÷ 5 Total Responses x 100 =

40% Conversion Rate

Campaign Profit

The total commission for this example shall be $15,000 per transaction. 2 Responses are resulting in Sales, which would bring the entire commission to $30,000. Assuming a 50/50 split between buyer and seller brokerage, and 1% marketing allowance ($1,500) to sell the listings, the result would be:

$13,500 in Net Profit Resulting from Campaign - $300 Campaign Expenses = $13,200 (Campaign Profits)

Return on Investment (ROI)

$13,200 Campaign Profits ÷ $300 (Cost of Campaign) = 44% ROI

Keep in mind that these numbers were calculated without consideration of any brokerage split between the brokerage and the individual agent and are purely hypothetical. You would still need to determine your own split before establishing your actual campaign profits and ROI.

THE 21ST CENTURY DIFFERENCE

Let's talk a little bit about technology and computer wizardry. But rest assured that mailers still work even without this part. However, I just didn't feel right excluding this part for the overall completion of this book. I said earlier, in order for you to have a lead, you need some form of contact information. The most common one people go after are email opt-ins. And the reason behind building an email list is simple: An email list is an asset to your business that you own and can decide what to do with later one. Let's contrast that with collecting page likes on Facebook. The page itself still belongs to Facebook. If I collect followers on Instagram, the account still belongs to Instagram. And for my business to be as bulletproof as possible, your email list can hold the keys to the kingdom. And there is also data evidence that suggests your income level is directly tied to the size of your email list.

According to BoomTown the stats are as follows:

- Up to 1,000 active subscribers - up to 14 Million
- 1,001-5,000 active subscribers - up to 20.4 Million
- 5,001-10,000 active subscribers - up to 30.9 Million
- 10,001-30,000 active subscribers - up to 44.9 Million
- 30,001-50,000 active subscribers - up to 81.4 Million

- 50,001-100,000 active subscribers - up to 124 Million
- 100,000+ active subscribers - up to & exceeding 220 Million

Building your email list can be very profitable for your bottom line, as well as the fact that people use their email to sign up for various social accounts. And what this means is a great way to know how to find your subscribers on other mediums, such as social media. Everytime you are creating a new account or registering somewhere online, you are asked to enter your email. Why? This is the most common identification/verification process used and with that offers you the perfect path to find your leads/subscribers online.

And this two-point verification form is still relying on email input. By having the email, it doesn't matter if the next big thing after MySpace is Facebook or Clubhouse or any other platform they're coming out with by the time I'm done writing this book. Once I have their email, I'll be able to identify them on any other platform with ease.

LANDING PAGES

Have you ever heard the statement: 'Many roads lead to Rome'? Well the same can be said about our website. And just as many places lead away from it. When a prospect is sent to our website, they typically are bombarded with a lot of options, such as : Buy, Sell, Blog, About Us, Search and more. How are we supposed to take control of their online journey like this? The answer is Landing Pages. A Landing Page is a site online that will only give them the option of one path to take. It is the most simplistic form of a website and in a world of stimulation and overwhelm a landing page can be a breath of fresh air. Let's take your CMA site as an example. When you send people to a free home evaluation site, it should only ask them to enter their address to receive their free CMA. We are not telling them about the Staging Guide we have or asking if they want to see our past client testimonials. We do not distract them with our new listings or ask if they want to browse a list of homes for sale. Our mission with a landing page is simple: One path for one result.

PIXELS/ANALYTICS

If you want to get really fancy, you could also make sure that your landing page has a tracking code installed. And while it is really easy to set it up yourself these days either with a Facebook Pixel or a Google Analytics code, there are also people that are able to help you with all this over on sites such as www.fiverr.com or www.freelancer.com. I am going to keep this chapter short because not everyone wants to dive in as deeply on the technology aspect. If you do want to dive in deeper on it, I suggest you check out our Facebook Group, the Hyper Local Real Estate Agent, and you're free to post any of your questions there as well.

QR CODES

The latest craze are QR codes. And I have personally used www.qrcode-monkey.com to generate mine, which is an absolutely free tool that you can check out. By adding a QR code to a mailer, a prospect can now take their phone, scan it, and it'll direct them to that site you want them to go to. I do urge you to consider who your mailer is aimed at. If the mailer is targeting impatient millennials that do not want to waste the time typing in a web address, this might be a great add-on to your mailers. If however your mailer is aiming to generate leads for retirement communities, this might be too far of a venture into the world of technology. Know your avatar and know the language they are speaking.

THE FAQS

Is direct mail really a successful strategy?

This is one of the things where I always refer back to the IRS. No, we're not talking about our taxes. We're talking about the fact that the IRS is simply not going to be emailing you. Strange, I know.

The IRS is purely relying on snail mail communication. Why is that? Well, for one, have you ever gone through your stack of mail and you were distracted with a phone in your hand? Probably not. Right? Every time I pick up my mail from the mailbox, I'll set it on the counter. And when I do go through it, I will need two hands, one to hold a letter and one to open it. I will sort the mail, but rarely is my attention split between social media or the television, or anything else going on in life. I am generally the most focused on the task at hand when it comes to going through the mail. Anybody else feel like this?

Here is another thing I want to point out. There are people in our industry sending 100,000+ mailers a month. I once asked, if direct mail is a successful strategy? The person laughed, shook their head and said, "Of course not." Which puzzled me. But here is the sentence that's followed next,

"I spent $300,000 a year on mailers because it doesn't work." Catch the sarcasm there? I hope you did. Just like open houses that can be mastered, so can mailers. And you dove deep on all the secrets to mailer marketing.

Most people will tell you, mailers are a waste of time, they don't work. And honestly, I want you to take those comments with a grain of salt. Most people that make these remarks may have sent a mailer or two, didn't see a return, and then thought, "I feel like it doesn't work." They base their judgment on a feeling. When it comes to business, I strongly suggest not to base your judgments off feelings. Track your numbers, and know what works. If you spend $1 on mailers and you get $2 out of it, that's a win. My current numbers are $1 out, and $10 out.

I don't know about you, but I would take those $9 gladly as profits. And just like any other lead generation tool, it is a number game. Let me give you another example: Social media advertisement. If I spend $1 on a Facebook ad, but I end up selling a $2 product, I come out ahead by $1.

One of my former mentors pointed out to me that everything works. However, most people are simply dabbling.

You try some open houses. You try some expired listings. Maybe some canceled listings. Send some mail to for sale by owners. Maybe door knock some of them, try geographic farming for a month or two. And, at the end, you wonder why nothing is working. The way I remember to become a master of my craft is by a simple statement. Jack of all trades, master of none. I now do not move on to implementing another strategy until I have mastered the one that I'm currently working on. And, when I say mastery, I mean mastery. I want to immerse myself in the topic, knowing my numbers, knowing what it means for me to be successful, knowing what exactly the steps are, systematizing it in order for me to hand it over to a third person so I can free up my time and immerse myself into a new strategy.

And, I applaud you for picking up this book. It means that you focused on doing exactly this. You are immersing yourself into a topic far beyond what other agents are willing to do. You're immersing yourself into a book, learning more and more about a lead gen strategy that can massively impact your business. One of the reasons I love mailers is for the fact that I get to do it after business hours. Bedtime rolls around my house and I get to design my mailer, send it off to the printer. The next morning, I get to make breakfast with my children knowing that my printing company is going to handle it from here during the normal nine to five hours while I go about my regular mom duties.

There is a second reason why I really love mailers. Mailers are highly scalable. When I first started out, I started out with 100 flyers, went to 400 mailers, now grew to 5,000 of them. And, I'm not planning on stopping. I can continue on with it, scale it as much as I need to in order for my business to grow while still being here for all my kids' milestones.

Will it work for me?

This has to be one of the most commonly asked questions that I hear. Will it work for my neighborhood? Will it work for my business? Will it work for my style of business? The biggest problem most agents face is the fact that they just simply give up too soon.

There's a graphic that comes to mind while I am writing this and it is an image of a miner who is heading back into his tunnel, all defeated, and he is only inches away from the treasure. A tunnel above him shows another miner who is absolutely eager, continuing on on his journey and getting closer to the treasure. The moral of the story? Never give up. Keep pushing forward and you shall receive at the other end of it. So, yes. Consistency is a huge part of this, but definitely not the only part.

Here's the truth. Mailers can work for everybody. However, there are a few things that I need you to be aware of. Simply sending mailers randomly is probably not the best strategy. If you are looking to send mailers, I suggest you identify the homes that you're going to be targeting based on a turn over rate.

What's the turnover rate? A turnover rate simply determines how many transactions are happening in your selected area, and if there are enough to support your income goal. Here is the formula for the turnover rate:

Total # of sales/year ÷ total # of homes in the area x 100= % Turnover Rate

A turnover rate should be anywhere from 5% to 10% for a profitable farm. So, here's a quick example:

A Neighborhood has 1500 homes that you are looking to target. In the last 3 years the subdivision had a total number of annual sales of:

Year 1: 94 sales

Year 2: 110 sales

Year 3: 103 sales

Based on these numbers the turnover rate would be as follows:

Year 1: 94 ÷ 1500 x 100= 6.27%

Year 2: 110 ÷ 1500 x 100= 7.33%

Year 3: 103 ÷ 1500 x 100= 6.86%

> **PRO TIP:**
> Go back more than 12 months (I typically recommend at least 3 years for my team members) to make sure the turnover rate is consistent over the years and wasn't caused by an unusual event such as a large corporation coming or leaving for example.

What if I don't have any money?

That's one of my favorite questions because when I got started, I literally had a zero dollar marketing budget. And, there's absolutely nothing wrong with starting out from zero. The question is, are you willing to invest your most valuable resource into your business? One of the things I always point out is the fact that we all have two resources and we need to draw from one or the other. Can you guess what these two resources are? The first one is time and the second one is money. We discussed these in the beginning of this book.

You will be investing either one of those resources in order to continue moving your business forward. When I got started, I invested time. I created flyers, printed them at the office and brought them around. So, can you use the strategy I am showing you in this book for mailers and put them on flyers? Absolutely. And instead of a mailer design, think in terms of a flyer design. And instead of money that you're investing to send mailers, think about your time that you're investing to deliver flyers. We are also still going to cover things such as vendors and third parties to make it more affordable. I went over my printing hacks and tips to make sure you're getting the best bang for your buck. This book is not only meant to educate you, but I hope I'll leave you with some really cool gold nuggets that save you money. For example, did you know that you can find stamps online for less than face value? These are prior year stamps you can find on sites such as eBay. Just make sure it is a reputable seller you are purchasing from.

Some people might call my approach cheap. I tend to call it cost effective. I'm a big believer that bad habits are created in good times. What does that mean? It means that many people are making an okay living and they're starting to invest massive amounts of money into glitzy, shiny objects that are not going to be needed in their business. Create a business as lean as possible with time/money in mind and you will find a high profit sweet spot.

What should I send?

I hope I gave you some ideas in my chapter on Lead Generation. I have included my TOP 10 Seller Mailers as well as suggestions for 2 years worth of a lead nurture campaign that you can utilize.

Where should you send mailers for the best results?

Really you could send mailers anywhere as long as you follow the math behind mailers and have a profitable farm. But there is also one other strategy you could use. Target hot commodity properties. What's that? These are the properties that will have the largest buyer pool in your area available. Determine the median sales price for your area. Let's assume a median sales price of $275,000 for this example. When it comes to farming, in order to appeal to the largest buyer pool possible, I would select farming in an area that is corresponding slightly under (-5%) and slightly above (+5%) this price point.

By doing so, you will increase your chances of more listings as well as attracting more buyers to you and your business. Of course, you can go after luxury properties, however, be mindful that there are a lot fewer of them and you also have fewer buyers. Your return is greater, but you want to keep in mind market time and what it would potentially mean for your paycheck if sales were to happen more sporadically. Your monetary investment up front is also typically higher with luxury properties.

If you already have a solid baseline established and a price point that you're comfortable with, maybe it is a great idea to look at the next up price point in order to inch up in price. But generally speaking, your biggest profits are typically to be had where the biggest buyer and seller pools are centered around.

Sending Mailers to New Construction Communities

I get asked time and time again on how to farm a new construction subdivision successfully. And here is the answer: Farming a New Construction Area can be extremely profitable as long as you approach it with a system that is the exact opposite of resale mailer marketing.

Did I confuse you yet? Here is the scoop: Resale neighborhoods already have an established turnover rate in which you can go in and full force start sending mailers for lead generation purposes. New construction communities are built in phases and if you are looking to get in on a subdivision in the ground-breaking years (year 0-2), you want to start sending Lead Nurture Mailers along with hosting events. Your initial turnover rate will be low (sure there might be the occasional relocation deal or divorce sale popping up, but generally speaking new construction takes some time to get going). So work on lead nurture campaigns if you are set on becoming the go to agent. Become the welcome community for your new neighbors (especially if they came into the community unrepresented by another agent and went directly through the builder!)

What if I don't live in an area I want to send mailers to?

This is another question I receive and the short answer is you approach it the same way as if you lived there. When I first started out looking at my neighborhood, I wasn't even aware that there are multiple subdivisions making up my community. I learned. I discovered what subdivision was built at what time. I researched floor plans, I researched schools because my children were too young to attend at that time, I researched small businesses, I researched parks. Discovering a new area has the same steps. Talk to local residents. Drive the neighborhood. Take a walk and discover the subdivision. There are many ways to get to know an area. I also like to do some sort of demographic review of the new area so I can tailor a message to the residents better for a higher offer opt-in. Do the mailers I send differ from my regular farm area? No they do not. Include their subdivision name on the mailer to speak directly to them for relevance.

Do I need to send a mailer every month?

I promised you this book was not about spending crazy amounts of money but to help you build a lean and profitable business while being there for your kids' milestones. I can honestly tell you that you can send mailers a lot less frequently. You can send a mailer every six weeks, for example, and you'll still be successful. When I first got started, I never sent more than six mailers in a year, yet I still gained market share.

Mailers need to be sent for 12 months before seeing a return

I've had students get leads on their very first mailing. So it's absolutely possible to turn a profit on mailing number one. I do think most people confuse the time spent to fully immerse yourself in a strategy and learn all possible things about it with the timeframe of how long you have to send mailers for initially to be successful. It will take some time to master mailers and after reading this book you are well on your way.

Sending mailers is complicated and I don't do where to start

Mailers are one of the easiest things to do, actually so easy that I still have enough brain power to do it after bedtime when my kids are in bed. So, believe me when I tell you, it's absolutely possible. The biggest obstacle is getting started with them. I do suggest checking out Mailer Mom - The System which shows you that sending mailers is truly as simple as 1-2-3. You can get the details at

www.MailerMom.com

CO-MARKETING OPPORTUNITIES - YOUR VENDORS

Who can be on a mailer with you? Co-branding is one of the greatest ways to make mailers more affordable for you as the agent. And one of the questions I get asked a lot is, "Who can be on the mailer with me?" And truth be told, anybody. So I want to just give you a few examples, but I want you to know that there are so many more possibilities.

The most commonly used service providers that are going on the mailer with us to share in on the cost are typically providers related around the real estate transaction. These vendors could include:

- Attorneys
- Lenders
- Title companies
- Inspectors

But there are others. You could also think about partnering up with local small business owners providing services related to a home such as:

- Window & Door companies
- Window cleaning company
- Cleaning service companies
- Renovation & Remodeling companies
- Handyman
- Plumber
- Electrician
- Roofer
- HVAC contractor
- Fire & Water Restoration Companies
- Waterproofing companies
- Carpet Cleaning Companies
- Landscape Design Companies
- Chimney Companies
- Insurance Agencies
- Sprinkler Companies
- Lawncare & Snow Removal companies
- And more

Those two categories are generally making the most sense for agents and you will find the least amount of pushback.

But that's not to say that you cannot partner with a dentist for example. Finding a connection between selling homes and the dentist might be quite tough but there are no rules telling you, you couldn't do this. And as long as there is a mutual benefit both of you could experience from it, I would suggest going for it and with it diverting the cost of mailer marketing.

CO-BRANDING AND COMPLIANCE

And the last thing I have for you in our nerdy chapter is compliance. I have copied here, from the official NAR page, the RESPA guidelines that you want to keep in mind when sending mail. As always, ask your brokerage for advice based on your state's guidelines and make sure you have the most up to date guidelines in front of you as a reference guide.

DO

- Do ensure that each co-marketing party pays its proper share of the advertisement.
    - Each party's share should be based on the proportionate split of the fair market value for any and all services in connection with the advertisement (e.g., creation, design, distribution, etc.); and
    - Each party's share should be equal to each advertised settlement service provider's prominence in the advertising.
- Do ensure that the agreed upon marketing is actually performed and that any payment made in connection with such services is the fair market value for the services performed.

- o Remember—just because a social media platform is "free" for users to join or post in, it does not mean that all uses of the platform are offered at no cost or that there are no costs associated with the development of the advertisement.
- o Be aware of what may constitute a thing of value, and remember it does not require a transfer of money. Any benefit or concession (a "quid pro quo") may be a "thing of value."
- Do include the word "Advertisement" in a prominent location on each party's information included on the co-marketing materials.
- Do document procedures to calculate co-marketing charges and/or create a standardized rate sheet for the fair market value of such marketing.
- Do consider maintaining written agreements of the co-marketing arrangement to demonstrate compliance with RESPA Section 8 as well as federal and state laws and regulations governing your comarketing efforts, including those regarding advertising, privacy, and licensing requirements, as applicable.
- Do ensure that the advertisements are distributed to the general public, such as publicly-facing, broadly-reaching websites, and cannot be viewed as "targeting" specific consumers.
- Do ongoing oversight of the co-marketing arrangement that may be required by either or both comarketing participants.

DO NOT

- DO NOT enter into the arrangement with a co-marketing party without getting the necessary corporate authorization for such arrangement for yourself or for your co-marketing party.
- DO NOT directly or indirectly defray expenses that would otherwise be incurred by anyone in a position to refer settlement services or business to you, by use of a co-marketing arrangement. Payments by settlement services providers to third party real estate listing aggregator sites that reduce your advertising costs can create a direct RESPA violation.
- DO NOT exchange any "thing of value" with anyone for a referral, no matter how small the "thing of value" is. RESPA does NOT have an exception for minimal "kickback" amounts and even a small amount (i.e., $5 coffee gift card) is considered a "thing of value" under the law.
- DO NOT require or allow your co-marketing party to endorse you, exclusively or otherwise, or vice versa, e.g.:
  - Do not allow either co-marketing party to refer to the other as a "preferred" service provider, or a "partner," or some other similar designation.
  - Beware of any perceived endorsements, such as "likes," follows, re-postings, tagged pictures with one another, and other favorable commentary on referral sources' pages, whether such activity is conducted from your personal or your business accounts. Remember that promotion of business

activities generally should be conducted from business accounts/pages, not personal ones.
- DO NOT enter into co-marketing arrangements before considering the implications of any other concurrent relationship with the co-marketing party (e.g., lead sales, desk rentals, etc.).
- DO NOT direct any of the co-marketing efforts to specific consumers with whom either co-marketing party has a relationship or over whom either party has the ability to influence the selection of a
- settlement service provider (as compared to marketing of general distribution)
- DO NOT evaluate or adjust the compensation paid under an arrangement based on "capture rate," which is the percentage of referrals that convert to actual clients or customers.
- DO NOT allow one party to act as a "gatekeeper" when dealing with a third-party marketing company. Both parties should have a separate agreement with third-party marketing firms.
- DO NOT perform services for the other co-marketing party that are outside the terms of the agreement. For example, if a real estate agent and a lender are co-marketing, the lender should not "incubate" or cull leads on behalf of the real estate agent as that is outside the terms of the comarketing agreement and is not a compensable service.
- DO NOT share the cost of leads generated through websites or arrangements. Each party must pay the fair market value of the leads they purchase.

*Disclaimer: This document is provided for

informational/instructional purposes only and does not constitute the giving of legal advice by NAR. Consult with a RESPA attorney to make sure you understand and properly comply with any and all applicable laws. As a reminder, some state and local laws prohibit or otherwise restrict activities that may be permissible under RESPA.

THE ULTIMATE TACTIC - A MAGIC PILL SOLUTION

Let's be honest, we are all looking for an easy way to gain more business and work less at the same time. And while there is not a magic pill per say, there is something called systems, processes and automations that I want to touch one so you can see the big picture and how it is all coming together! And on that note, I also want to say: Congratulations, you made it to the very last and final part of this book. I know we covered a ton and I only want to hint on those as the purpose of this book is not to give you an entire overview of all the systems that you can have. But I want you to understand that a successful real estate business is thriving based on the following systems: a customer relationship management tool (CRM), email marketing software and leverage.

CUSTOMER RELATIONSHIP MANAGEMENT (CRM)

A CRM is literally the most amazing thing you could potentially have in your business. Okay, I can't believe I actually just said that but it really is the backbone of a successful business. And I know many agents are not a fan of their CRM. Let me start by saying that I think if you are not in love with your CRM, you probably have the wrong CRM. Most people simply use the one from their brokerage. The brokerage will provide a CRM and the agent will look at it and then decide not to use it because they don't find it appealing. If this is you, I suggest you do a little bit of research on CRMs. And I also wanted to share with you my five must do things that any CRM should do.

MUST HAVE FEATURES:

1. You must be able to add leads manually and automatically into your CRM
2. The ability to add notes to each individual lead inside your CRM
3. The ability to create Types & Categories to organize: Buyers/Sellers/Leads/Clients/Past Clients/etc.
4. Mass email feature so you can send one email to everyone in your database all at once as well as Drip Email
5. Manual and automatic Tasking feature

Your CRM is very much like a personal assistant, somebody that keeps track of everything that needs to happen, keeps track of conversation and everything else related to your real estate business. Let me give you an example of one of the ways I use my CRM and how it has created business opportunities that have paid me more than I can count by simply having it in place. Every time I close a transaction, I close out a file in my CRM and put up follow-up tasks in place. These follow-up tasks include check-in with my clients quarterly.

It also reminds me to reach out to them on their home anniversary as this is a special time that they and I share and that's connecting us. After doing hundreds of transactions, I can honestly tell you I am beyond grateful to have a system that reminds me when they're home anniversaries are coming up. There is no way that I would be remembering when I closed what transaction. Now I simply got a reminder from my system on their special day to reach out to them and wish them a happy home anniversary. This is invaluable.

And if you are not having a CRM in place, I honestly would love for you to check out the one I'm using as it is a checklist-friendly one. I have added this to the resource section along with my referral link for you.

EMAIL MARKETING

The second thing I want to talk about is your email marketing. As you may have noticed, I'm mainly using my mailers for lead generation, which means that I am offering them something of value in exchange for their email address, a form of getting a contact.

Email marketing in itself has so many valuable points that I simply needed to include this one. Most agents are afraid to email their database too many times. Just think about Kohl's or Best Buy or even Amazon. There have been days when I do receive 3+ emails from them. Crazy, yet I remain with them because I will use them when I have the need for them and simply delete my emails from them until then.

LEVERAGE

Creating relationships does take time and personally I love adding leverage to my life and business anywhere I can, so that I am able to enjoy the things in life that make it all worth it. For me, those are the milestones with my kids, the outings and getaways to reconnect. I think Gary Keller highlighted Leverage in his book 'The Million Dollar Real Estate Agent' in such great detail that it is worth checking out. For me leverage was essential for growth. Lead data input can be handled by an administrative assistant. Video Editing was passed off to an editor once the budget was in place. Groceries are getting delivered through Instacart. Our life is consumed with tasks. It is your choice which ones you are wanting to take on to make the most sense to you. And this again is a scenario of Not one size fits all. You design your life based on what you want it to look like.

For the sake of efficiency and reconnecting with as many people as possible in your database, I want to highlight two possible ways to accomplish this. The first one is to host Open Houses as a way to invite potential leads from your database. This eliminates the one to one reach outs to set an appointment and takes the pressure of the lead as well. The second option could be an event you are hosting for your sphere or neighborhood or both. I have successfully hosted events such as Pictures with The Easter Bunny, Neighborhood Garage Sales, Food Drives, Graduation Parades and more and it allowed me to connect with as many people as possible in the shortest amount of time! I told you the motto I live by is "Efficiency is where the Profit is!"

For more information on neighborhood events to become a geographic-dominating agent, You can also check out the Hyper Local Real Estate Agent Facebook Group that has all the resources for many of our events. And you will find a community of like-minded people ready to build their empires.

I'm cheering for you!

For access to all the free Resources and Trainings mentioned in this book, please go to:

www.MailerMomResources.com

CHAPTER 5
RESOURCES

RESOURCES

Join us inside our Facebook Group:

The Hyper Local Real Estate Agent

Access my free Resources and Trainings mentioned in this book at www.MailerMomResources.com

TOOLS

Background Remover
www.remove.bg

QR Code Generator
www.qrcode-monkey.com

Xpressdocs (Printing)
www.xpressdocs.com

Remine (Tax Record Service & Printing)
www.Remine.com

Vistaprint (Printing)
www.Vistaprint.com

Website with people for hire that have a skill you are looking for

www.Fiverr.com

Website with people for hire that have a skill you are looking for

www.freelancer.com

My CRM

www.insightly.com

My Email Provider

www.Mailchimp.com

COURSE

Dominate your geographic Farm with Direct Mail and 3x your reach without increasing your budget

www.bit.ly/MailerTraining

My favorite EDDM Template to use

(Download all of them in the free Resource Section at www.MailerMomResources.com)

Front
6.25x9

SIZE FOR DESIGN:
6.5 X 9.25

BLEED: Extend all background color and images to the red bleed line.

TRIM : Final cut line. Text or background should not end at the blue trim line.

Mailer Mom

Back
6.25x9

PRSRT STD
ECRWSS
U.S.POSTAGE
PAID
EDDM Retail

*************ECRWSS****

Local
Postal Customer

BLEED: Extend all background color and images to the red bleed line.

TRIM: Final cut line. Text or background should not end at the blue trim line.

Mailer Mom

Remember to register for my next free Bootcamp

Mailer Mom - The free 5-Day Bootcamp

This is a free Training that I host!

There is No Cost, but I only run the bootcamp a few times a year!

So don't wait to get in on the next one!

"How to get your First (or Next) Successful Real Estate Mailer designed and sent off to print in less than a week WITHOUT paying Expensive Third Party Services and Finally Generate Real Leads on Demand!"

This Works Even if you have never sent a Mailer for Generating Buyer & Seller Leads Before!

REGISTER NOW FOR THE NEXT BOOTCAMP!!

www.MailerMomBootcamp.com

Walk through the exact steps I take to get a new successful Mailer generated that sets listing appointments for me without dragging people through a sales pitch!

Made in the USA
Middletown, DE
14 December 2022